實用漢語課本

Practical Chinese Reader II
Patterns and Exercises

New and Revised

Traditional Character Edition

漢字作業簿

繁體字本

陳 凌 霞

Ling-hsia Yeh

About the Author

Ling-hsia Yeh is an assistant professor of Chinese in the Department of Asian Languages and Literatures, University of Massachusetts, Amherst. She received her B.A. degree in Foreign Languages and Literatures from National Taiwan University, and her M.A. and Ph.D. degrees in linguistics from Indiana University.

1995 Printing

Cheng & Tsui Company
25 West Street
Boston, MA 02111-1268 USA
e-mail ct@world.std.com

Library of Congress Catalog Control Number: 93-074711

New and Revised Traditional Character Edition 0-88727-200-2
New and Revised Simplified Character Edition 0-88727-208-8

Companion textbook, writing workbooks, computer software, video tapes and audio tapes are available from the publisher.

Printed in the United States of America

PUBLISHER'S NOTE

The Cheng & Tsui Company is pleased to announce the most recent volume of the *C&T Asian Language Series,* the new and revised edition of *Practical Chinese Reader II: Patterns and Exercises.* This workbook supplements the highly successful introductory Chinese language textbook *Practical Chinese Reader II,* compiled by the Beijing Language Institute.

In this new and revised edition you will find that the original text for *Patterns and Exercises II* has undergone some minor changes; essentially, the same intensive, systematic study of the basic grammatical structure of Chinese remains. However, Professor Ling-hsia Yeh has appended three different indices to her workbook: Appendix One is a Chinese-Pinyin-English index; Appendix Two is an English-Chinese-Pinyin index; and Appendix Three is a Stroke Number index.

The C&T Asian Language Series is designed to publish and widely distribute quality language texts as they are completed by teachers at leading educational institutions. *The C&T Asian Language Series* is devoted to significant works in the field of Asian languages developed in the United States and elsewhere.

We welcome readers' comments and suggestions concerning the publications in this series. Please contact the following members of the Editorial Board:

NOTE ON THE SECOND EDITION

Except for a few places where some corrections have been made, the contents of this edition are essentially the same as those of the first edition. However, the reader may find useful the three appendices which are newly added. The typing of the three appendices is supported by part of a Faculty Research Grant from the University of Massachusetts at Amherst. I am appreciative of Mr. Tong Shen and Mr. Shaodan Lo for their meticulous work of typing the draft of the appendices.

CONTENTS

PREFACE

This workbook was written with the intention of providing a companion to the textbook *Practical Chinese Reader: Book II,* compiled by the Beijing Language Institute. Although it is meant to be a sequel to *Practical Chinese Reader I: Patterns and Exercises* by Professor Madeline Chu of Kalamazoo College, Michigan, it does not entirely follow the format and approach adopted in her book.

The organization of the workbook is such that for each lesson, except review lessons, there is a grammar review followed by a set of exercises. The grammar review attempts to provide an overall presentation of the grammar and sentence patterns in every lesson. A certain portion of the exercises are designed to reflect those patterns and their usages. The students are then required to decide what to use and when to use their knowledge of the grammar in the related exercises. The grammar notes follow as closely as possible the explanations in the textbook, with the exception of lessons 39 and 47, where certain verb-type words are considered as post-verbal prepositions rather than resultative verb complements.

The goal of the exercises is to familiarize students with the vocabulary, sentence structure, and content of every lesson. There are generally four to five exercises in each lesson. The forms frequently employed include fill-in-the blanks, word-order, question and answer, sentence completion, structural change, and translation. The arrangement of the exercises for each lesson is such that practice on vocabulary comes first, followed by those on structure and content, with the translation exercises at the very end, since they require knowledge of both vocabulary and grammar.

Not many compositional exercises are included since they can always be assigned by individual instructors to serve their own needs. The compositional exercises given in this workbook are controlled ones in the sense that vocabulary and sentence structure for writing the compositions are controlled within the limit of related lessons. At the same time, students are still allowed to stretch their imaginations.

A few words must be said about some of the English sentences in the translation exercises. Although they may not sound idiomatic, those sentences are written deliberately either to correspond to the structures of their Chinese counterparts or to give clues to certain Chinese structures. This is done to avoid the possibility of coming up with misleading translations for the exercises.

The author welcomes comments and suggestions from users of this volume. This author alone is responsible for any mistakes that may be found in this book.

– Ling-hsia Yeh
University of Massachusetts, Amherst
January 1991

ACKNOWLEDGEMENTS

I am grateful to the Five Colleges East Asian Languages Program for providing me with a grant which made possible the completion of this work in its present form.

I should like to express my sincere appreciation to the following people for their assistance and encouragement:

Members of the Editorial Board of the Cheng & Tsui Company's *Asian Language Series* for their comments and suggestions for revising the manuscript;

Professor Donald Gjertson for going over the translation exercises and for polishing the sentences;

Professor Shou-hsin Teng for his encouragement and generous loan of the Chinese computer software program used in producing this work;

Ms. Jiaxiang Dai for typing the translation exercises.

I should like to express special thanks to Mr. Tong Shen, a Ph.D. candidate in the linguistics department of the University of Massachusetts, Amherst for typing, editing and printing the manuscript numerous times. Without his patience and meticulous work, the final draft would not have been completed in its present form.

Finally, I would like to thank my colleagues, and especially Nina Rose-Racine, of the Department of Asian Languages and Literatures for their moral support.

– Ling-hsia Yeh
University of Massachusetts, Amherst

ABBREVIATIONS

Adjective	Adj
Adverb	Adv
Aspect	Asp
Interrogative Pronoun	IP
Negation	Neg
Noun Phrase	NP
Object	Obj
Other Element	OE
Preposition	Prep
Question Device	QD
Subject	Subj
Stative Verb	SV
Verb Phrase	VP

Note: Words with asterisk following them are those given in the supplementary vocabulary lists.

Practical Chinese Reader #31 Grammar Notes

Interaction between time-measure complements (TMC) and verbal -了 as well as the sentential 了

I. Regular pattern

A. Verbs without objects

1. Habitual or future events

Subj (+ OE) + Verb + TMC
他 每天 學習 兩個小時。
(He studies for two hours every day.)

2. Past events

Subj (+ OE) + Verb + -le + TMC
他 昨天 鍛煉 了 一個小時。
(He exercised for an hour yesterday.)

王老師 在中國 住 了 三個月。
(Professor Wang stayed in China for three months.)

3. Events which took place in the past and have been carried into the moment of utterance

Subj (+ OE) + verb + -le + TMC + le
我 已經 學習 了 兩個小時 了。
(I have been studying for two hours.)

B. Verbs with objects

1. Habitual or future events

Subj (+ OE) + Verb + Obj + Verb + TMC
他 想 學習 漢語 學習 一年。
(He intends to study Chinese for a year.)

2. Past events

Subj (+ OE) + Verb + Obj + Verb + -le + TMC
他 在中國 學習 漢語 學習 了 一年。
(He studied Chinese in China for a year.)

3. Events which took place in the past and continued to the moment of utterance

Subj (+ OE) + Verb + Obj (+ OE) + Verb + -le + TMC + le
他 在中國 學習 漢語 已經 學習 了 一年 了。
(He has been studying Chinese in China for a year.)

II. Insertion pattern

This pattern applies to sentences with non-specific verbal objects and only if the objects are not pronouns.

Subj	(+ OE) +	Verb +	(-le) +	TMC +	(de) +	Obj +	(le)
他	想	學習		兩年	的	漢語。	
(He intends to study Chinese for two years.)							
他	昨天	看	了	一個小時	的	電視。	
(He watched television for an hour yesterday.)							
我	已經	坐	了	十個小時	的	飛機	了。
(I have been on the airplane for ten hours.)							

III. The usage of 多 with a numeral

A. When the numeral is 'ten' or less

Numeral +	Measure +	多 +	Noun
三	個	多	小時

B. When the numeral is 'ten' or more

Numeral +	多 +	Measure +	Noun
三十	多	個	小時

C. Exceptions: 天 and 年 behave like measure words.

三年多
四天多
三十多年
二十多天

Practical Chinese Reader #31 Exercise A

Fill in appropriate vocabulary:

1. 你在這兒住了多長 ___ ___ 了?

2. 你學了 ___ 年中文了?

3. 1965年我 ___ 二次回中國，參觀了很多工廠。

4. 北京是中國的 ___ ___ 。

5. 一天有二十四個 ___ ___。

6. 去中國以前我們先要去辦 ___ ___ 。

7. 北京的機場是一個 ___ ___ 機場。

8. 中國是一個 ___ ___ 主義的國家。

9. 中國希望 ___ ___ 四個現代化。

10. 我的媽媽很 ___ ___ ，每天工作十個小時。

11. 在外國住了很久的中國人叫 ___ ___ ___ 。

12. 希望你們能 ___ 國家作一點事。

13. 我在上海住了三 ___ 多月。

Practical Chinese Reader #31 Exercise B

Word order:

1. 我　回國　1963年　第一次

2. 我　住了　在　三個多月　上海

3. 你家裡　在北京　有人　還　嗎

4. 我　三十　教書　已經　多　了　年　教了

5. 學生代表　是　北京　的　語言學院　我

6. 坐　飛機　你們　多長　了　時間　的

7. 不錯　北京　真　天氣　的

8. 我弟弟　兩年　準備　學習　在中國　多

9. 有　中文系　老師　位　十　多

10. 到北京　十分鐘　有　還　要　就　了

Practical Chinese Reader #31 Exercise C

Complete the following sentences with phrases containing time-measure complements.

1. 我們三點鐘到國際機場，現在六點半，朋友還沒來，我們等他已經 ________________________.

2. 他九點十分去買東西，九點五十五分開車回家．他 ____________ 的東西．

3. 我的朋友今年夏天要去中國學習漢語，他想明年冬天回美國． 他準備在中國 ________________________.

4. 昨天我們早上十點坐飛機，中午十二點半到那個大城．我們 ________________________.

5. 我們每天上午十點十分上漢語課，十一點五分下課． 我們每天 ________________________漢語課．

6. 1965年王老師開始在外語學院教書． 他現在已經 ________________________.

7. 我每天晚上十一點睡覺，早上七點起床． 我每天 ________________________.

8. 那些代表們晚上七點開始開會*，現在九點四十分． 他們 ________________________.

Practical Chinese Reader #31 Exercise D

Translate into Chinese (using regular pattern):

1. How many hours do you work every day?

2. He lived in the capital for half a year.

3. I hope I will be able to stay in China for three months.

4. How long did that overseas Chinese visit that factory?
More than two hours.

5. That student representative has been waiting for him for twenty minutes.

6. How many months has he lived in the countryside?
More than four months.

7. They did not watch TV for the whole evening. They only watched for a half hour or so.

8. Are you going to use the car for a long time?
I will use it for three days.

9. Prof. Wang has been teaching in that college for over thirty years.

10. I have been on the plane for more than ten hours.

Practical Chinese Reader #31 Exercise E

I. Translate into Chinese (using insertion pattern):

1. How long have you been riding on the train?

2. They watched movies for two hours and forty minutes.

3. The students have been holding a meeting for the whole evening.

4. Twenty some teachers shopped for one and a half hours yesterday.

5. This overseas Chinese intends to study Chinese for one year and a half.

II. Translate the following dialog:

A: Haven't seen you for a long time. Where have you been?
B: I went to China for three months.
A: Was it the first time that you went to China?
B: No, it was the second time.
A: Is there anyone in your family who lives in China?
B: Yes, my older brother.

I. The experiential aspect marker 過

Subj (+ Neg/OE) + Verb + Asp + NP (+ QD)
我 最近 看 過 那個電影。
(I saw that movie recently.)

我 沒(有) 看 過 那個電影。
(I have never seen that movie.)

你 看 過 那個電影 嗎/沒有?
(Have you ever seen that movie?)

II. Verb-過 and frequency

A. An expression of frequency follows a verb and its aspect marker.

Subj (+ OE) + Verb + Asp + Frequency
我 去年 透視 過 兩次。
(I had X-ray examination twice last year.)

B. Insertion pattern is more frequently used when a verb is followed by a general noun (i.e., a non-specific noun).

Subj + Verb + Asp + Frequency + Obj
我 看 過 兩次 中國電影。
(I have seen Chinese movies twice.)

C. When the object of a verb is a pronoun or an expression of location, insertion pattern is not allowed.

我去過他家一次。
(I have been to his home once.)

我弟弟見過他兩次。
(My younger brother has seen him twice.)

D. When the object of a verb is a definite noun, it is always topicalized (i.e., placed at the beginning of a sentence) and frequency therefore follows the verb.

那個電影我看過兩遍。
(I have seen that movie twice.)

Practical Chinese Reader #32 Exercise A

I. Fill in blanks with appropriate vocabulary.

1. 我去大學 ____ ____ ____ 看病。

2. 我的心臟不太好，請給我 ____ 一下血壓吧！

3. 你第一 ____ 來中國嗎？ 不，我 ____ 二次來.

4. 我們去醫務所 ____ ____ 身體.

5. 我沒 ____ 過什麼大病. 七歲的時候，得 ____ 一 ____ 肺炎.

6. 檢查身體以前，請先到那兒拿一 ____ 表.

7. 那個中國電影，他已經看過兩 ____ 了.

8. 他最近去過兩 ____ 北海.

9. 那個足球隊贏過三 ____，也輸 ____ 三次.

10. 這個漢字，我寫過兩遍了，我要 ____ 寫一 ____.

11. 有人說 "有志者事竟成"。我以前也聽過 ____ ____ 的話。

12. 爸爸媽媽給我們 ____ ____。 老師給我們 ____ ____ 。

Practical Chinese Reader #32 Exercise A

II. Identification.

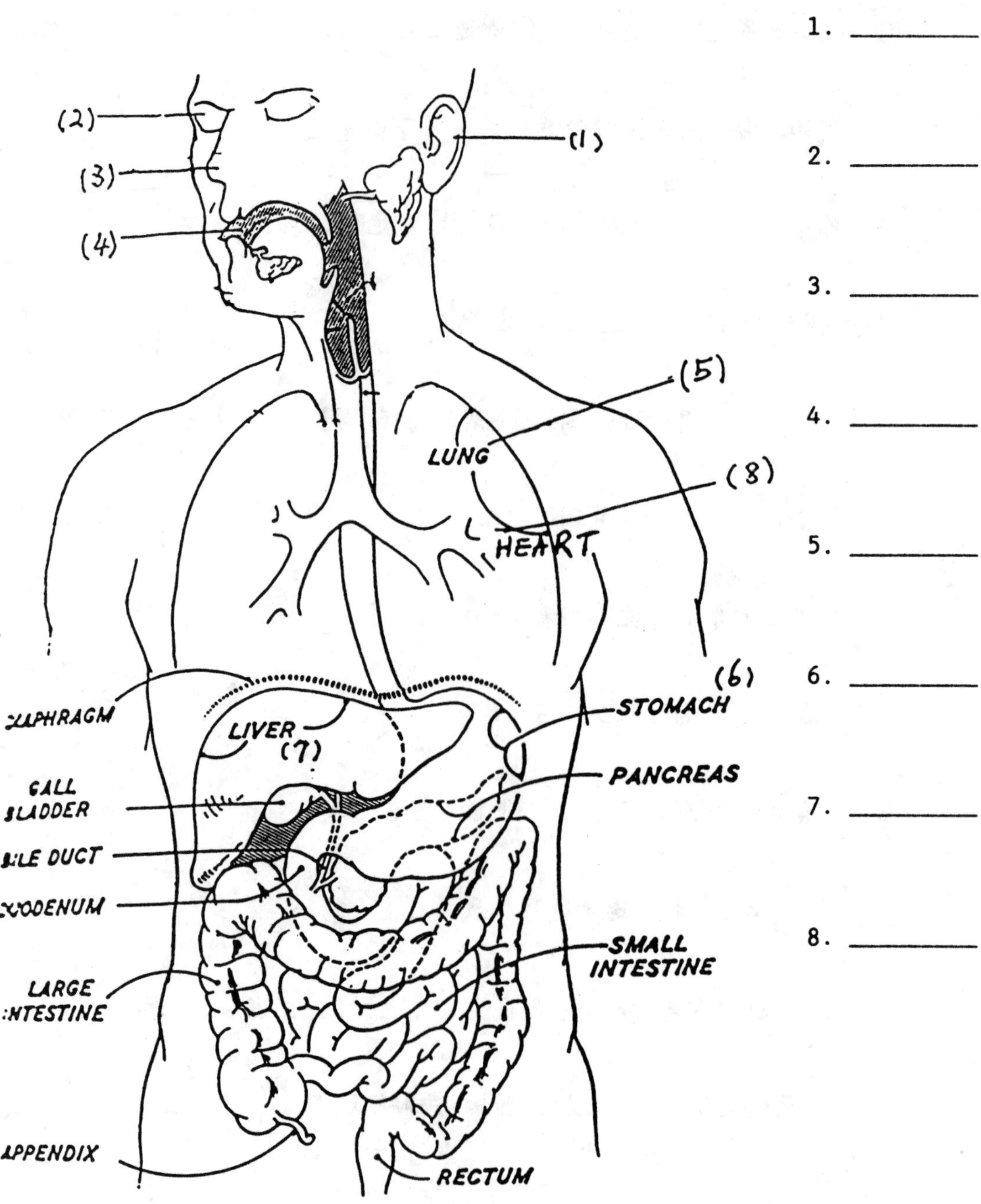

1. ________

2. ________

3. ________

4. ________

5. ________

6. ________

7. ________

8. ________

Practical Chinese Reader #32 Exercise B

Fill in blanks with 了, 過 or 0 (=nothing).

1. 這個練習，我已經看 ____ 一遍 ____，不會有錯.

2. 你以前用 ____ 筷子嗎? 我沒用 ____.

3. 我們七點吃飯，他來 ____ 沒有? 他還沒來 ____ 呢.

4. 這件襯衫太小 ____，我不想買.

5. 他們來 ____ 北京一個多星期 ____，參觀 ____ 很多地方.

6. 對 ____，我十歲的時候去 ____ 英國，在那兒住 ____ 三個月.

7. 你會用 ____ 毛筆寫 ____ 中文嗎?

8. 他看電視已經看 ____ 兩個小時 ____.

9. 那本書我已經唸 ____ 兩遍 ____.

10. 我昨天沒復習 ____ 課文，我忘 ____ 今天有漢語課.

11. 他來 ____ 找 ____ 你三次.

12. 我們就要 ____ 去 ____ 中國訪問.

Practical Chinese Reader #32 Exercise C

Word order:

1. 血壓　一下　去　他　量　醫務所

2. 電視裏　中國電影　幾次　我　在　看過

3. 心臟　血壓　和　我的　正常　都　嗎

4. 透視　到　請　一下　對面房間　吧

5. 還　我　一遍　這個電影　看　想

6. 可以　以後　透視　就　了　走

7. 要　我希望　自己　鍛煉　注意　你

8. 小時候　病了　得過　我　兩個月　肺炎

9. 你　拿一張表　内科　再去　先在那兒　量血壓

10. 哪些地方　來北京　星期　了　你們　過　一個
    去　多

Practical Chinese Reader #32 Exercise D

Translate into Chinese:

1. Have you seen this movie before?
   No, I have never seen it.

2. My father has had a physical check-up recently.

3. Have you ever had a serious illness?
   I had pneumonia when I was ten years old.

4. How many times have you had your blood pressure measured?

5. Have you ever seen a doctor at that infirmary?
   Yes, I have seen doctors there three times.

6. Last year his mother had an X-ray examination once.

7. I have listened to this song several times. I would like to listen to it once more.

8. How many times have you read that (literature) book?

9. How many times have you been to that place?
   I have been there four times.

10. Please take a look at this form.

11. We asked them to tell us about Beijing for a while.

12. I have never heard such saying before.

13. Before you see the doctor, go to the internal medicine department first to get a form.

I. Sentential particle 了 which occurs at the end of a sentence may indicate a change of state.

A. Sentences with stative verbs (or adjectival predicates)

Subj	(+ OE)	+	SV	+	le
天氣			冷		了。

(It is getting cold.)

樹上的葉子	都		紅		了。

(All the leaves have turned red.)

雨			小		了.

(The rain is letting up.)

B. Sentences with nouns as their predicates

現在十點了，我們回家吧。
(It is ten o'clock. Let's go home.)

這個孩子今年十二歲了。
(The kid is twelve years old now.)

C. Sentences with meteorological verbs which are always subjectless

下雨了。 (It is raining.)

刮風了。 (It is windy.)

D. Sentences with 'verb to be', 'verb to have', modals, and non-adjectival type stative verbs

現在他是大學生了。 (He is a college student now.)

他有工作了。 (He has a job now.)

我會說漢語了。 (I can speak Chinese now.)

II. The construction 不...了 also indicates a change of state. It implies that a circumstance no longer exists.

不下雪了。 (The snow has stopped.)

Practical Chinese Reader #33 Exercise A

Fill in blanks with appropriate vocabulary.

1. 有人 ____ 門，請你去開門，好嗎?

2. 春天來 ____，花園裡的花都 ____ 得很好.

3. 這兒的冬天很冷，時間也很長，常常 ____ 風，____ 雪.

4. 秋天的時候，樹上的 ____ ____ 都紅 ____，大家都喜歡去看紅葉.

5. 張老師教我們一 ____ 古詩.

6. 梅花不 ____ 冷，也不怕雪. 文學家 ____ 梅花寫 ____ 不少詩.

7. 天氣預報* ____ 明天會下雪.

8. A. 北京的天氣 ____ ____ ____ ?

   B: 不錯.

9. 那兒的夏天天氣很熱，最熱的時候到過一百 ____.*

10. 五分鐘以前還下雨，現在雨 ____ 了.

11. 今天冷嗎? 我不 ____ ____ 很冷，我覺得很暖和.

12. 那兒的天氣很好，天天 ____ 是晴天.

Practical Chinese Reader #33 Exercise B

Word order:

1. 公園 玩兒 今天天氣 很好 你們 嗎 沒到

2. 有人 很熱 夏天 告訴我 北京的 以前

3. 秋天 樹上的 了 紅 葉子 現在是 都 了

4. 梅花 大風 天氣 大雪的 很好 開得 在

5. 今天 到 寫了 梅花 文學家 爲 不少詩 從古時候

6. 冬天 在 有 花 什麼 中國

7. 晴天 下雨 現在是 今天上午 了

8. 常常 冬天 北京的 刮風 下雪

9. 我們 時間不早 以後 談 了 吧 再

10. 那本書 你 的 要 這是

Practical Chinese Reader #33 Exercise C

Complete the following sentences:

1. 下雪的時候，這兒很漂亮．你應該 ________________________.

2. 這兒的夏天很熱，我以前不習慣，現在 ________________________.

3. A：他告訴我他要去檢查身體．

   B：不，他有事兒，他 ________________________.

4. 現在是春天了． ________________________.

5. 秋天到了， ________________________.

6. 冬天來了， ________________________.

7. 我以前很喜歡喝咖啡，現在 ________________________.

8. A：你再坐一會兒．

   B：不， ________________________.

9. 雨停了， ________________________.

10. 我弟弟以前不會游泳， ________________________.

Practical Chinese Reader #33 Exercise D

Translate into Chinese:

1. What time is it (now)?
   It is nine o'clock now. We shall set off pretty soon.

2. It is spring (now). All the flowers are in blossom.

3. It was raining when I came this morning. It is snowing (now).

4. It is summer (now). The weather is getting hotter.

5. Has the rain stopped?
   No, it is still very heavy.

6. He told me that he was going to have a physical check-up today.
   No, he is busy. He will not go.

7. My younger brother is a college student (now). He can drive (now).

8. I liked swimming when I was young, but I do not like it any more.

Practical Chinese Reader #33 Exercise E

Translate into Chinese:

1. We watched football game on TV from 2:30 till 4:45.

2. A: Is it far from here to his house?

B: Not far. It only takes ten minutes to get there.

3. A: Someone told me that winter in Beijing is long. The lowest temperature ever is ten degrees centigrade below zero.

B: That's right. I think that spring in Beijing is best. The weather is really nice. It is neither cold nor hot. It is sunny everyday.

A: I heard that the Summer Palace is beautiful in summer.

B: But it is even more beautiful when there is snow.

Practical Chinese Reader #33 Exercise F

Write a paragraph describing your reading of the cartoon.

Practical Chinese Reader #34 Grammar Notes

The aspect marker 著 indicates a continued state. Possible cases employing the aspect are as follows.

A. An action verb followed by 著

Subj (+ Neg) + Verb + Asp (+ NP) (+ QD)

他 拿 著 一封信。

(He is holding a letter.)

那個女孩子 穿 著 一件紅襯衫 嗎/沒有?

(Does that girl wear a red blouse?)

營業員 沒 看 著 書。

(The clerk was not reading a book.)

B. The state of an inanimate subject

房間裡的燈沒開著。

(The light in the room was not on.)

學校的門開著沒有?

(Is the gate of the school open?

C. When a locative expression is the focus of a sentence

Location (+ Neg) + Verb + -zhe + NP (+ QD)

牆上 掛 著 一張圖片。

(A picture was hung on the wall.)

牌子上 沒 寫 著 漢字。

(Chinese characters were not written on the sign.)

櫃台上 放 著 郵票 沒有?

(Were stamps placed on the counter?)

D. Structures with serial verbs where 著 is attached to the first verb to form a verbal phrase describing the manner in which the second verb is performed.

Subj (+ OE) + Verb1 + Asp (+ NP1) + Verb2 (+ NP2)

他們 站 著 寫 信。

(They stood while writing letters.)

我 喜歡 喝 著 咖啡 聽 音樂。

(I like to drink coffee while listening to music.)

Practical Chinese Reader #34 Exercise A

Fill in blanks with appropriate vocabulary.

1. 這個房間的窗户前邊 ____ 著一張床。 床上 ____ 著一本書。床下 ____ 著一雙鞋。牆上 ____ 著一張畫兒。畫上 ____ 著梅花。 旁邊還 ____ 著一首詩。

2. 外邊有兩個人，都 ____ 著大衣。兩人手裡都 ____ 著帽子。

3. 包裹裡邊裝* ____ 一 ____ 帽子和兩 ____ 襯衫。

4. 他熱情 ____ 說："我會認真 ____ 學習。"

5. 王老師笑 ____ 對我說："我很高興你能到中國去學習。"

6. 我不知道這 ____ 信是誰寄的。 信封上沒寫 ____ 寄信人的姓名。

7. 我去他家的時候，他正打 ____ 電話呢！

8. 公園裡邊有很多人，有的坐 ____ 說話，____ ____ 玩著球。

9. 在郵局、商店裡工作的人我們叫他們 ____ ____ ____。

10. 我想很快 ____ 告訴他這個新聞，我不知道我應該 ____ 信還是 ____ 電報。

11. 我到郵局去 ____ 一封信。

12. 營業員給我七 ____ 郵票，二十 ____ 信封。

Practical Chinese Reader #34 Exercise B

Word order:

1. 一個　牌子　牌子上邊　掛着　寫着　窗口前邊　字

2. 郵局里的　營業員　大聲　地　問　你　買什麽　要

3. 要　郵局　航空信　給　朋友　去　我　寄

4. 明信片　郵票　和　櫃台里邊　放　很多　着

5. 姓名　地址　你的　和　下邊　要寫　還要

6. 醫務所　一張表　拿　他　去　檢查　着　身體

7. 食堂里 有的 吃飯 人很多 坐着 站着 有的　買菜

8. 上課的時候 注意地 他 學習 下課的時候　認真地
他　聽

9. 很多電影 有的 有的 喜歡 不喜歡 看過 我　我　我

10. 圖片　字　寫着　没　爲什麽　上

Practical Chinese Reader #34 Exercise C

Answer the following questions:

1. 你的房間住著幾個人?

我的房間住著六個人.

2. 你喜歡坐著看書還是站著看書?

-0.05 我喜歡坐著看書.

3. 寄英文信的時候，寄信人的姓名和地址在信封上邊還是在信封下邊?

-0.1 英文信有寄信人的姓名和地址在信封上邊。

4. 在中國寄中文信的時候，收信人的地址在信封上邊還是在信封下邊?

在中國寄中文信的時候收信人的地址在信的上邊.

5. 寄航空信快還是寄平信快?

6. 本市的郵局每天開幾個小時?

郵局每天開八個小時.

7. 每天上課的時候來得晚的人，以後應該怎麼樣?

8. 你打過中文電報* 沒有?

9. 從這兒到你家的信要多少天?

10. 你爲什麼學習漢語?

Practical Chinese Reader #34 Exercise D

Translate into Chinese:

1. The clerk wore a new shirt. He was holding a postcard in his hand.

   營業員穿着新襯衫. 他手上拿着明信片.

2. Was the TV in the living-room on?
   No, it wasn't on.

   客廳的電視開嗎? 沒開着

3. A table was placed in front of the window.

   一個桌子放在窗前邊

4. Many beautiful stamps were placed inside the counter.

   很多漂亮的郵票放在櫃台的裏邊着.

5. A plate was hung on the wall.

6. Is the door of the post office open?
   Yes, it is open.

7. I like to drink coffee while I listen to music.

8. He answered with a smile: "The sender's name and address have to be written at the bottom."

9. He said while pointing to the chart: "You should write the envelope this way."

10. There are many people in the post office. Some are waiting to buy stamps. Some are sitting and writing letters.

Practical Chinese Reader #34 Exercise E

Translate into Chinese:

1. While in class, the students listened attentively.

2. He said loudly to me: "Let's go swimming."

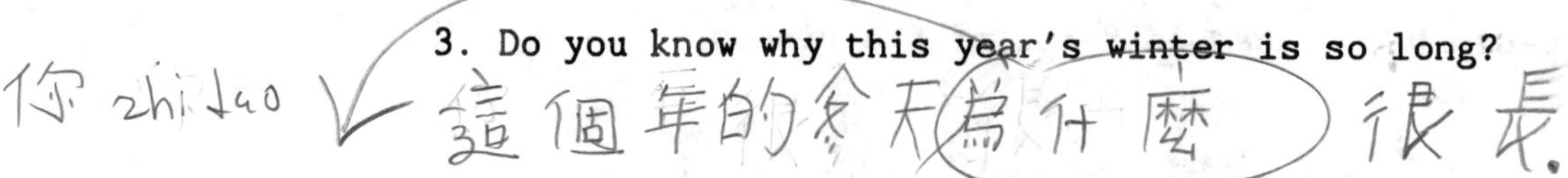

3. Do you know why this year's winter is so long?

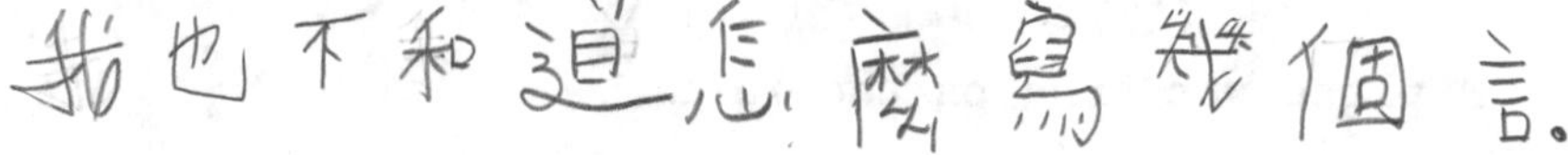

4. I still do not know how to write some of these words.

5. Some people like to see movies; some like to listen to music.

6. My friend has many stamps. Some are Chinese ones; some are foreign ones.

7. A: Excuse me, how long does it take to send a letter to China?
   B: Regular mail or air mail?
   A: Air mail.
   B: It takes a week.
   A: I want to have it registered too.

Practical Chinese Reader #35 Exercise A

Fill in blanks with 着，了，在 or 過.

1. 行李上沒有寫 着 他的名字.

2. 現在梅花正開 着 呢.

3. 我還沒用 過 筷子吃中國菜.

4. 五月十五日就要考試 了，考試以後就放暑假 了.

5. 他以前當 過 老師，現在不當 了.

6. 他笑 着 說："我在這兒已經住 過 了 兩年 了."

7. 這個字我們學 過，可是我又忘 了.

8. 我弟弟穿 着 冰鞋正 在 滑冰呢.

9. 你在這兒照相 過 沒有?

(or 過)

10. 你在那個食堂吃 了 飯沒有?

11. 我昨天去看他的時候，他 在 看電視呢.

Practical Chinese Reader #35 Exercise B

Fill in blanks with 再，又，還 or 就.

1. 放了假，我 就 坐飛機回家了.

2. 今年寒假我工作了一個月，掙了一些錢. 我想利用暑假 再 掙點錢.

3. 上星期我的錶停了，後來好了. 今天我的錶 又 停了.

4. 我們今天考試了，明天 還 要考呢.

5. 我們吃飯以後 再 談吧.

6. 外邊 還 下雨呢!

7. 那個電影我看過兩次. 我想 再 看一次.

8. 快十二點了，他 還 不想睡.

9. 這一次考試，我考得不好. 我想 再 復習一下這一課.

10. 我現在不給家裡寫信. 我想放假了 ~~再~~ 就 寫.

11. 雨已經停了，我們 就 要回去了.

Practical Chinese Reader #35 Exercise C

Answer the following questions:

1. 你的專業是什麼?

我的專業是学生. It has to be a field, not a position

2. 這學期你給家裡寫過幾次信?

專

我没有給家裡寫信。

3. 要口語進步應該怎麼樣?

-0.05

我不知道應該麼怎樣。樣

4. 你説中國話的機會多不多?國

我説中國話的機會多。

5. 你們什麼時候放暑假?

五月我們放暑假.

6. 今年暑假你想作什麼?

我想去法國.

7. 你們下學期幾月開學?

一月我們要回學校。

8. 你了解中國的情況嗎?

我不了解中國的情況.

9. 你們多長時間考一次試?

我們每個星期考試 試

10. 你學習了漢語以後想作什麼?

學習了漢語以後我想去中國.

Practical Chinese Reader #35 Exercise D

Translate into Chinese:

1. They took an examination on the fourth day after arriving in Beijing.

2. Some of the students did well in the examination; some did a bit worse.

3. I feel that my speaking skill is not very good. I want to practice listening and speaking more.

4. He made great progress. He can talk with his friends in English now.

5. I was afraid that my parents would be worried. I have written them twice.

6. He used to work in the post office, but he doesn't work there any more.

7. It's December now. We are about to have the winter break.

8. He has been sick for three days. His mother is worried.

9. The doctor carefully checked his heart and said with a smile: "Your heart is normal."

10. I intend to study Chinese for a year here, then I will go to China.

Practical Chinese Reader #36 Grammar Notes

I. Comparative structures with the preposition 比

A. Comparison is made between two objects with regard to a certain quality which is expressed by a stative verb or a verbal phrase.

Subj1 + bi + Subj2 + SV/VP
他 比 我 忙。
(He is busier than I am.)

我 比 我朋友 了解中國。
(I have better understanding of China than my friend does.)

B. Structures with adverbials of degree
(b's are possible but less frequent.)

1. a. Subj1 + Verb + de + bi + Subj2 + SV
他 跑 得 比 我 快。
(He runs faster than I do.)

b. Subj1 + bi + Subj2 + Verb + de + SV
他 比 我 跑 得 快。
(He runs faster than I do.)

2. a. Subj1 + Verb + Obj + Verb + de + bi + Subj2 + SV
他 作 菜 作 得 比 我 好。
(He cooks better than I do.)

b. Subj1 + Verb + Obj + bi + Subj2 + Verb + de + SV
他 作 菜 比 我 作 得 好。
(He cooks better than I do.)

Note: The negative form 不比 is rarely used out of context. It is often used to negate an assertion.

Eg. X: 我想他跑得比你快。
(I think he runs faster than you do.)

Y: 不，他跑得不比我快。
(No, he doesn't run faster than I do.)

II. Comparative structures with 有/沒有

The negative form is used more frequently while the positive form is only used in context.

A. Subj1 + meiyou + Subj2 + SV/VP
這間房間 沒有 那間房間 大。
(This room is not as big as that one.)

我 沒有 他 喜歡音樂。
(I don't like music as much as he does.)

B. Structures modified by adverbials of degree
(b's are possible but less frequent.)

1. a. Subj1 + Verb + de + meiyou + Subj2 + SV
他 跑 得 沒有 我 快。
(He doesn't run as fast as I do.)

b. Subj1 + meiyou + Subj2 + Verb + de + SV
他 沒有 我 跑 得 快。
(He doesn't run as fast as I do.)

2. a. Subj1 + Verb + Obj + meiyou + Subj2 + Verb + de + SV
我 作 菜 沒有 他 作 得 好。
(I don't cook as well as he does.)

b. Subj1 + meiyou + Subj2 + Verb + Obj + Verb + de + SV
我 沒有 他 作 菜 作 得 好。
(I don't cook as well as he does.)

Practical Chinese Reader #36 Exercise A

I. Give appropriate measure words.

1. 一 ____ 茶具

2. 四 ____ 茶壺

3. 兩 ____ 茶碗

4. 這個工廠不生產這 ____ 瓷器.

5. $5.96 = 五 ____ 九 ____ 六 ____

6. 一 ____ 畫兒

II. Fill in blanks.

1. 這套茶具比那 ____ 便宜.

2. 這種紙沒有那 ____ 薄.

3. 他游泳比我 ____ 得快.

4. 百貨大樓的東西比這家商店 ____ 多.

5. 我弟弟畫畫兒畫 ____ 沒有我好.

6. 這個茶碗不 ____ 那個高.

7. 你的自行車 ____ 他的高嗎? 我的沒有他的高.

8. 這種冰鞋一 ____ 多少錢?

9. 這種明信片多少錢一套? 一塊三 ____ 六.

10. ____ 比這套便宜的嗎? 沒有, 這套最便宜.

Practical Chinese Reader #36 Exercise B

Rewrite the following sentences by using the worde given in parentheses.

1. 昨天很冷. 今天更冷. (比)

2. 這個售貨員二十三歲. 那個售貨員三十歲. (比)

3. 這種瓷器薄. 那種瓷器更薄. (不比)

4. 唐山生產瓷器的歷史很長. 景德鎮生產瓷器的歷史更長. (沒有)

5. 這種自行車的質量好. 那種自行車的質量也好. (有)

6. 他每天六點起床. 我每天七點起床. (沒有)

7. 他複習了五課課文. 我複習了三課課文. (比)

8. 我弟弟寫字寫得好. 我妹妹寫字也寫得好. (有)

9. 他進步得快. 我進步得慢. (不比)

10. 我喜歡看電視. 我朋友更喜歡看電視. (沒有)

Practical Chinese Reader #36 Exercise C

Word order:

1. 瓷器　玉　白　紙　薄　那兒的　比　比

2. 質量　提高了　以前　這種茶具的　比

3. 我的　没有　他的　歷史知識　多

4. 兩個　我　茶壺　要　的　五元

5. 這種表　那種　便宜　有　嗎

6. 很長　景德鎮　瓷器　的　歷史　生産

7. 六個茶碗　一共　四十二　塊　毛　四

8. 漂亮　比　這套明信片　有　的　嗎

9. 比　他　開車　我　開得　好

10. 我　她　喜歡音樂　没有

Practical Chinese Reader #36 Exercise D

Translate into Chinese:

1. This bicycle is cheaper than that one.

2. This kind of jade is not as thin as that kind.

3. Is the quality of this kind of china better than the quality of that kind?

4. Is this tea set as good as that one?

5. Is there anyone in your class who is younger than you are?

6. The painting on this tea pot is prettier than the painting on that one.

7. Things in the Department Store are more expensive than those in this shop.

8. Is England's history longer than China's?

9. My friend studies harder than I do.

10. This college football team does not play as well as that one.

Practical Chinese Reader #36 Exercise E

Translate into Chinese:

1. He sings better than I do.

2. My younger sister does not read as many history books as I do.

3. This sales clerk speaks English better than that one.

4. This factory manufactures more tea cups than that one.

5. I do not paint as well as he does.

6. The teachers did not come as early as the students did.

7. A: How much are the postcards per set?
   B: $3.95 per set.
   A: I want two sets. How much are they altogether?
   B: $7.50 for two sets.
   A: Here is a ten dollar bill.
   B: Here is your change, $2.50.

I. Comparative structures expressing equivalence

A. Subj1 + gen + Subj2 (+ bu) + yiyang (+ SV)
這種布 跟 那種布 一樣。
(This kind of material is the same as that kind of material.)

今年的天氣 跟 去年 不 一樣。
(This year's weather is different from last year's.)

他 跟 我 一樣 忙。
(He is as busy as I am.)

B. Subj1 + Verb + Obj + Verb + de + gen + Subj2 + yiyang (+ SV)
他 説 漢語 説 得 跟 中國人 一樣。
(He speaks Chinese like a native speaker.)

他 説 漢語 説 得 跟 中國人 一樣 好。
(He speaks Chinese as well as a native speaker does.)

II. Comparative structures with complements of quantity which can be non-specific as 一點兒 ('a little'), 得多 ('much more'), 一些 ('a little'), or specific.

Subj1 + bi + Subj2 + SV + quantity
今天 比 昨天 冷 一點兒。
(Today is a bit colder than yesterday.)

這種布 比 那種布 好看 一些。
(This kind of material is a little prettier than that kind.)

他弟弟 比 他 年輕 得多。
(His brother is much younger than he is.)

這種筆 比 那種 便宜 五塊錢。
(This kind of pen is five dollars cheaper than that kind.)

III. A difference in quantity or time from what was originally planned or expected may be expressed by the adverbs 多, 少, 早, 晚 occurring before verbs and quantity.

我多花了十塊錢。
(I spent ten dollars more.)

他少買了一張電影票。
(He bought one less movie ticket.)

我只比你早來了五分鐘。
(I came only five minutes earlier than you did.)

你先走吧，我要晚走一刻鐘。
(You go first. I'll leave fifteen minutes later.)

Practical Chinese Reader #37 Exercise A

Fill in blanks with appropriate vocabulary.

1. 這件中山裝跟那件 ____ ____ 肥，可是不 ____ ____ 長. 那件比這件長五公分.

2. 我的棉襖的 ____ ____ 跟你的不一樣. 我的是藍的，你的是灰的.

3. 這件衣服的 ____ ____ 合適嗎？ 不 ____ ____，太短了一些.

4. 這件外衣比那件長 ____ ____？ 這件比那件長三公分.

5. 這種綢子多少錢一 ____？ 三塊八一米.

6. 這輛自行車跟那 ____ 一樣新嗎？ 不，那 ____ 舊一點兒.

7. 這件雨衣長70公分，那件長72公分. 這件比那件 ____ 兩公分.

8. 他的錶現在是一點五分，我的錶是一點十分. 我的錶比他的 ____ 五分鐘.

9. 他花了二十塊錢，我花了二十五塊. 他比我 ____ 花了五塊錢.

10. 這種茶具十五塊一套， 那種三十塊一套. 這種茶具比那種 ____ ____ 得多.

11. 這雙布鞋合適嗎？ 小 ____ ____. 再試試這雙.

12. 他吃一個麵包，我吃兩個麵包. 我比他多吃 ____ ____.

13. 他哥哥二十歲，他十八歲. 他比他哥哥小 ____ ____ .

Practical Chinese Reader #37 Exercise B

Word order:

1. 我　一樣　高　我朋友　跟

2. 三天　只　多　比　平信　寄　寄　航空信

3. 中山裝　藍色　穿　我　的　有　嗎

4. 錢　我　哪兒　應該　交　在

5. 便宜　比　布面的　綢面的　二十塊　錢

6. 好　多　我　他　得　游得　游泳　比

7. 瘦　比　我妹妹　我　一點兒

8. 肥　跟　這件　那件　衣服　不一樣

9. 兩瓶　酒　太多了　請少買

10. 一年中文　比　好　我　只學了　說得　可是　他

Practical Chinese Reader #37 Exercise C

Answer the following questions:

1. 你穿多大號的衣服?

2. 你穿幾號鞋?

3. 你有多高?

4. 你穿的外衣是中式的，還是西式的?

5. 你喜歡什麼顏色?

6. 你爸爸比你媽媽大嗎? 大幾歲?

7. 這兒的天氣跟你家那兒一樣不一樣? 哪兒比較暖和?

8. 你有綢面的中式棉襖嗎?

9. 你説漢語説得跟中國人一樣嗎?

10. 你家的車是什麼顏色的?

Practical Chinese Reader #37 Exercise D

Translate into Chinese:

1. The color of this cotton tunic suit is the same as that one.

2. The length of this cotton-padded jacket is not the same as the black one.

3. Is the weather here same as the weather in your country?

4. This jacket fits as well as that one.

5. Does he ride a bicycle as fast as you do?

6. Did you spend as much money as he did?

7. This sales clerk speaks English like an Englishman.

8. How much is this kind of fabric per meter?

9. These Western-style suits are $119 per set.

10. The bicycles are $89 each.

Practical Chinese Reader #37 Exercise E

Translate into Chinese:

1. This Chinese style cotton-padded jacket is a little bit shorter than that one.

2. The blue sweater is much more loose-fitting than the red one.

3. This kind of silk fabric is five dollars more expensive than that kind.

4. The custom-made table is five centimeters higher than the one you bought.

5. The kind of material I bought is a bit thicker than the kind he bought.

6. This time I paid ten dollars less than last time.

7. My friend spent twenty dollars more than I did.

8. Last month, this factory manufactured one hundred bicycles more than before.

Practical Chinese Reader #38 Grammar Notes

I. Resultative verbs are normally made of two verbs. The first element indicates an action and the second element describes the result or outcome of the first verb. The second verb always has a fixed meaning. Following are some examples.

1. 好: in a good state; properly -- 放好 (to put properly); 作好 (to do something well); 記好 (to remember well)

2. 錯: wrong; by mistake -- 説錯 (to say something wrong); 聽錯 (did not hear the correct message); 看錯 (did not see correctly)

3. 對: correctly -- 作對 (to do the right thing); 説對 (to say something correctly); 拿對 (to get the right thing)

4. 懂: to understand -- 聽懂 (to listen and understand); 看懂 (to understand through reading or seeing);

5. 見: to perceive -- 看見 (to see); 聽見 (to hear)

6. 會: to acquire a skill -- 學會 (to master)

Since a resultative verb always describes the result of an action, i.e., it refers to a completed or expected to be completed event. imperfective aspect marker 著 therefore never cooccurs with it. 了 is the most likely aspect marker to be employed.

Subj	(+ Neg)	+ Verb	+ Comp	(+ Asp)	+ NP	(+ le)	(+ QD)
他		看	懂	了	這封信。		
(He read and understood this letter.)							
我	沒	看	見		他。		
(I did not see him.)							
他		學	會		開汽車	了	沒有?
(Has he learned how to drive a car yet?)							

II. Expressions of direction

往 + Direction + Verb

往 前 走。 (Go straight ahead.)

往 右 拐。 (Turn to the right.)

Practical Chinese Reader #38 Exercise A

Fill in blanks with appropriate vocabulary.

1. 請問，到語言學院 怎 麼 走?

2. 從這兒 往 南走，到紅綠燈再 往 右拐.

3. 買兩張 ____ 平安里的票.

4. 我要坐開 ____ 北海公園的車.

5. 換13 路 公共汽車，在哪兒下車?

6. 這路車的終點 ____ 是平安里.

7. 鋼鐵學院 ____ 這兒遠不遠?

8. 這個字很容易，你 ____ ____ 沒寫對?

9. 請問這是什麼 ____ ____ ?　這是東邊.

10. 上課以前請先 ____ 隊.

Practical Chinese Reader #38 Exercise B

Fill in blanks with appropriate resultative complements:

1. 下飛機的人請帶 ____ 自己的行李.

2. 今天上午的考試不難，老師的問題我都回答 對 了.

3. 我學中文學了快一年了，我能看 好 容易的中文書.

4. 今天我不能開車，我的汽車還沒修 好 呢!

5. 有人敲門，你聽 ____ 了沒有?

6. 昨天你在學校看 ____ 了我哥哥沒有?

7. 他說漢語說得不清楚，我沒有聽 ____.

8. 去中國以前，你要先到中國大使館去辦 ____ 簽證.

9. 收信人的地址不對，你寫 ____ 了.

10. 我還沒學 ____ 開車，所以我不能開車送你去車站.

11. 我們寫 ____ 練習以後再去看電影吧!

12. 這路車不去百貨大樓，你坐 ____ 了.

13. 這個成語故事你聽 ____ 了沒有?

Practical Chinese Reader #38 Exercise C

Translate into Chinese (using resultative verb complements):

1. The bus is about to start. Please be seated properly.

公共汽車

2. I did not hear correctly the address he gave me.

3. Did you do the exercises correctly?

4. The clerk did not understand (through reading) the characters on the sign.

5. Have you seen the jacket I am looking for?

6. The worker has repaired his bicycle.

7. Sorry I'm late. I took the wrong bus.

8. This question is pretty easy. How come he didn't answer it correctly?

9. How come he didn't understand (by listening) the ticket-seller's questions?

10. I haven't learned how to use chopsticks.

Practical Chinese Reader #38 Exercise D

Translate into Chinese:

1. A: Excuse me, how do I get to the department store?
   B: Go south from here. Make a left turn when you get to the traffic lights.

2. A: Where is the street-car station?
   B: Go west. Make a right turn at the intersection.

3. A: Two tickets for the Language Institute.
   B: You've taken the wrong bus. The direction is not right. You should take the bus which goes east.
   A: What number bus should I take?
   B: You get off at the park and transfer to number 113 bus.

4. A: How many more stops are there before the terminus?
   B: There are three more stops. Please take your things with you when getting off.

5. A: Does this bus go to the Beijing Iron and Steel Engineering Institute?
   B: Yes. Please line up to get on the bus.

Practical Chinese Reader #38 Exercise E

Gubo (古波) went to see his friend yesterday. Write a short paragraph describing how he got to his friend's house in accordance with the given chart.

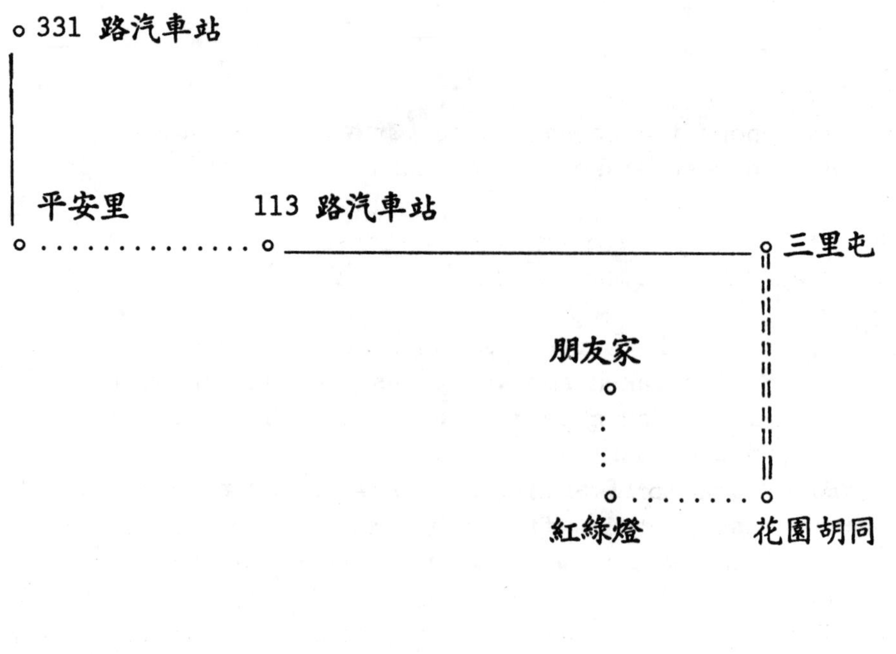

———— 坐公共汽車

.... 走路

======== 坐電車

Practical Chinese Reader #39 Grammar Notes

I. More resultative verbs!

1. 到 -- to succeed in
   找到 (to find); 收到 (to receive); 見到 (to see); 拿到 (to get)

2. 完 -- to finish
   唱完 (to finish singing); 用完 (to finish using)

3. 住 -- in a fixed or proper state
   記住 (to remember well)

II. Post-verbal prepositions

Post-verbal prepositions are certain verb type words which occur immediately after the main verb in a sentence. These verbs should not be considered as resultative complements, because they are more closely related to the noun phrases following them than to the preceding verbs. They may indicate a location or a recipient. Thus they behave more like pre-verbal prepositions or coverbs such as 從, 在, 到, 把, or 用.

1. 在 -- at, on, in
   放在 (to put in/on/at); 寫在 (to write ... on); 掛在 (to hang on)

2. 到 -- to
   走到 (to walk to); 學到(第三十課) (to study to lesson 30)

3. 往 -- toward
   開往 (to drive toward)

III. Fronting of definite noun phrases

When a verb with a definite noun phrase as its object is followed by the post-verbal preposition 在, the object is fronted to the beginning of the sentence in which it occurs. For example:

那套明信片我放在桌子上了。
(I placed the set of postcards on the table.)

今天的練習我寫在紙上。
(I wrote today's exercises on the paper.)

IV. Sentence connectives

A. The construction 一 ... 就 ('as soon as') functions as a connective associating two sentences. Both 一 and 就 must precede a verb. If the subjects of the two sentences are identical, the second one may be deleted.

Subj1	+ yi +	Predicate1	(+ Subj2)	+ jiu +	Predicate2
我	一	放假		就	回國。

(I will return to my country as soon as the vacation begins.)

他	一	教	大家	就	會了。

(Once he started teaching, everyone learned.)

B. 雖然 ... 但是/可是 -- although ... but

雖然他沒來過中國，可是對北京了解得很多。
(Although he has never been to China, he knows a lot about Beijing.)

他雖然沒來過中國，但是對北京了解得很多。
(Although he has never been to China, he knows a lot about Beijing.)

Practical Chinese Reader #39 Exercise A

I. Fill in blanks with proper verbs and resultative complements.

1. 上午我去宿舍找他，可是沒 ______ 他.

2. 上個月我阿姨説要從中國給我來信，我昨天 ______ 她的信了.

3. 我可以用你的詞典嗎?

   可以，但是 ______ 了請放在我的書桌上.

4. 我媽媽到百貨大樓去買那種茶具，可是沒 ______，因爲他們沒有那種茶具.

5. 我在哪兒辦手續?　在那兒. ______ 了手續請到對面透視.

6. 老師講的語法，我記了，可是沒 ______，都忘了.

7. 今天下午大學隊和工人隊賽球. ______ 了以後，大家一起去吃飯.

II. Fill in blanks with proper main verbs and post-verbal prepositions.

1. 我的帽子在哪兒?　你的帽子 ______ 牆上呢!

2. 他的名字，我 ______ 本子上了.

3. 昨天晚上我作練習 ______ 十二點鐘.

4. 這學期我們學了很多課漢語. 我們現在 ______ 第三十九課了.

5. 你要的那本書我沒帶來，我 ______ 家里了.

6. 請問，到郵局怎麼走?　你 ______ 紅綠燈以後，往右拐.

7. 我的外衣，你放好了嗎?　我 ______ 箱子裡了.

Practical Chinese Reader #39 Exercise B

Word order:

1. 鄰居 我們 很關心 對 我們的

2. 的 意思 嗎 成語 懂 你 這句

3. 了 天氣 是 雖然 春天 還是 現在 很冷 已經 但是

4. 弟弟 的 是 叔叔 爸爸

5. 在街上 還能 他 可是 做一些工作 雖然 退休了 已經 他

6. 愉快的 我們 記住 一天 這個 永遠 要

7. 笑 小姑娘 了 客人 就 看見 一 這個

8. 吃飯 留 客人 下來 請 遠方的

9. 上月 車間主任 當了 他 車間里選舉

Practical Chinese Reader #39 Exercise C

Answer the following questions according to the content of the text in this lesson.

1. 古波和帕蘭卡上星期去丁雲家，他們見到了丁雲家裡的什麼人?

2. 丁雲她爸爸作什麼工作?

3. 丁雲的媽媽現在怎麼樣?

4. 帕蘭卡爲什麼說丁雲家的鄰居也非常熱情?

5. 小蘭是誰?　她今年幾歲?

6. 丁雲爸爸怎麼說他自己?　那句話是什麼意思?

7. 丁雲媽媽留古波和帕蘭卡吃飯，他們留下來了沒有?　爲什麼?

8. 那一天古波和帕蘭卡過得很愉快.　對那一天，他們要怎麼樣?

Practical Chinese Reader #39 Exercise D

Translate into Chinese:

1. A: Listen! Someone is knocking at the door.
   B: I didn't hear it.

2. A: Did you receive letters from your uncle?
   B: No. But I received a letter from my aunt this morning.

3. A: Have they finished studying this book?
   B: Not yet.

4. This student did not memorize the vocabulary well.

5. I've looked for my notebook all morning, but I didn't find it.

6. Have you received the bicycle he gave you (as present)?

7. It was pretty late when I walked to the station.

8. We have already studied up to lesson thirty.

Practical Chinese Reader #39 Exercise E

Translate into Chinese:

1. I put the notebook you bought on the table.

2. Where did you write your neighbor's address?

3. The guests left as soon as we finished eating. Nobody stayed.

4. As soon as he heard this piece of news, he cried.

5. As soon as the retired teacher returned to his home, he saw his younger sister running to the street to welcome him.

6. Although he is smart, he does not understand the meaning of this sentence.

7. Although he said that he would remember that day forever, he soon forgot it all.

Practical Chinese Reader #40 Exercise A

Fill in blanks with sentence particles 呢, 吧, or 了.

1. 現在是夏天 <u>了</u>, 天氣已經很熱 <u>吧</u>.
2. A: 今年秋天你要回國 <u>吧</u>?

   B: 不, 我不回國, 我還要在中國住半年 <u>呢</u>.
3. A: 我們在哪兒下車 <u>呢</u>?

   B: 我們在終點站下車 <u>吧</u>.
4. A: 別看電視 <u>吧</u>, 現在已經七點 <u>呢</u>, 電影快開始 <u>了</u>.

   B: 你先走 <u>吧</u>, 我不想去看電影 <u>了</u>.
5. A: 昨天晚上他們在家作什麼 <u>呢</u>?

   B: 我去的時候他們正看電視 <u>呢</u>.
6. A: 他們已經拿到表 <u>了</u>, 你們 <u>呢</u>?

   B: 我們也拿到 <u>了</u>.
7. A: 再吃點 <u>吧</u>.

   B: 謝謝, 我已經吃得很多 <u>了</u>.
8. 我們還沒見過面 <u>呢</u>. 你是學生代表王小藍 <u>吧</u>?
9. 運動會就要開始 <u>了</u>. 觀眾都站在操場旁邊, 可是主席還沒到主席台上 <u>呢</u>.
10. A: 這次的百米賽他一定能打破記錄, 你 <u>呢</u>?

    B: 不, 我能保持記錄就很好 <u>了</u>.

Practical Chinese Reader #40 Exercise B

Fill in blanks with resultative complements.

1. 有人敲門，你聽 __見__ 了沒有？

2. 他激動地說："網球賽已經打 __完__ 了，我輸了."

3. 觀眾們鼓 __完__ 了掌以後，主席開始說話了.

4. 他跑到百米的終點那兒的時候看 __見__ 了很多觀眾站在那兒.

5. 你聽 __到__ 廣播了嗎？沒有，太遠了，我沒聽 __到__.

6. 那個運動員跑得快極了，他打 __破__ 了男子百米賽的記錄.

7. 這是誰的錶？別拿 __走__ 了.

8. 這一課的生詞你都記 __得__ 了嗎？

9. 他找 __到__ 了他的照片了沒有？

10. 我每天洗 __了__ 澡以後才吃早飯.

11. 今天早上他去接他的叔叔，接 __到__ 了沒有？

Practical Chinese Reader #40 Exercise C

Answer the following questions:

1. 你喜歡什麼運動?

我喜歡游泳.

2. 夏天最好的運動是什麼?

夏天最好的運動是游泳.

3. 你参加過運動會嗎?

我没参加過.

4. 你會不會打太極拳?

我會打太極拳.

-0.1 5. 看運動比賽的時候你激動嗎?

我覺得那種比賽不有激動.

6. 你有沒有你爸爸高?

我没有我爸爸高.

7. 今天是不是比昨天冷?

8. 你説漢語説得跟你的老師一樣好嗎?

9. 你常常聽新聞廣播嗎?

10. 作完這個練習以後你要作什麼?

Practical Chinese Reader #40 Exercise D

Translate into Chinese:

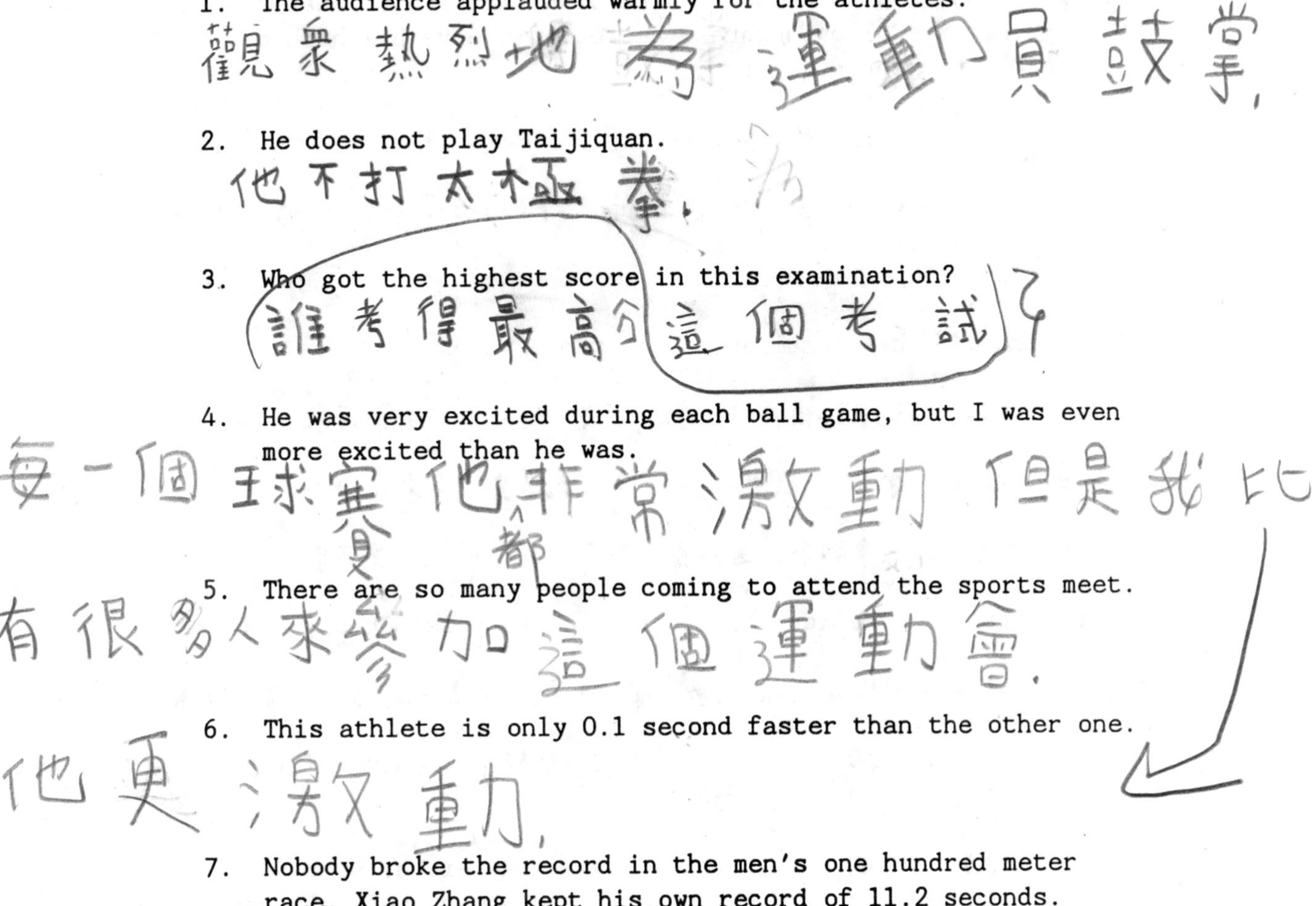

1. The audience applauded warmly for the athletes.

2. He does not play Taijiquan.

3. Who got the highest score in this examination?

4. He was very excited during each ball game, but I was even more excited than he was.

5. There are so many people coming to attend the sports meet.

6. This athlete is only 0.1 second faster than the other one.

7. Nobody broke the record in the men's one hundred meter race. Xiao Zhang kept his own record of 11.2 seconds.

8. The athletic field at our school is much bigger than the one at their school.

9. Who is the fastest runner in this sports meet?

10. The tea set she bought is the same as the tea set you bought, but hers was cheaper than yours.

I. Verbs with directional complements: A full-fledged verbal phrase with a directional complement comprises three verbs -- V1 V2 V3. V1 normally indicates action; V2 indecates position; V3 expresses direction (toward or away from the speaker). Following are examples of the verbs which may fall into different groups.

V1: 拿，帶，跑，走，寄，送，買，找，請

V2: 進(in)，出(out)，上(up)，下(down)，回(back)，過(over)

V3: 來，去

There are possible combinations of these verbs.

A. V2V3: 進來，出去，上來，下去，進去，回去，過來，etc.

B. V1V3: 拿來，跑去，走來，寄去，送去，買來，帶去，etc.

C. V1V2V3: 拿回來，送過去，帶進去，走出來，買過來，etc.

If the verb takes an object, there are two possible structures.

D. V1 + O + V3: 打電話來，帶照相機去，寄一封信去，帶行李來

E. V1 + V3 + O: 打來電話，帶來一位嚮導，買來吃的東西，送去一本詞典

II. 要是 ... 就 (if ... then): 要是 may either precede or follow a subject while 就 always occurs before a verb.

1. yaoshi + Subj1 + Predicate1 + Subj2 + jiu + Predicate2
要是 你 每天都鍛煉，你的身體 就 會很健康。
(If you exercise everyday, you will be very healthy.)

2. Subj1 + yaoshi + Predicate1 + Subj2 + jiu + Predicate2
他 要是 不來， 我們 就 去找他。
(If he does not come, we will go to see him.)

III. Contrast between 才 and 就: A sentence with 才 expresses an event which does not live up to one's expectation, therefore 才 never cooccur with Asp -了. A sentence with 就, on the contrary, indicates events exceeding one's expectation.

他八點才來。 (He didn't come until eight o'clock.)

他八點就來了。 (He came as early as eight o'clock.)

Practical Chinese Reader #41 Exercise A

I. Fill in blanks with appropriate vocabulary.

1. 昨天我們去長城玩，小張 ___ 我們帶來了一位嚮導.

2. 那個亭子高高地站在山上，___ 人一樣.

3. 每天上午到學院的車都很 ___，車上的人多 ___ 了，很多人都沒有座位.

4. 我八點從家裡 ___ 來，在路上 ___ 了半個小時才到這兒.

5. 我哥哥研究中國歷史，他 ___ 中國很了解.

6. 天安門是一個高高的 ___ ___，前邊有一個 ___ ___.

7. 我聽 ___ 《李自成》是一本有名的 ___ ___，說的是崇禎 ___ ___ 在景山山 ___ 下吊死的故事.

8. 我們在門口等了一 ___ ___，他就進來了.

9. A: ___ ___ ___，我來晚了.

   B: ___ ___ ___，我們也剛到.

II. Fill in blanks with directional complements 來 or 去.

1. 嚮導和我們都在車上，你快上 ___ 吧.

2. 照相機在樓下. 你下 ___ 拿吧.

3. 我哥哥從中國寄 ___ 了一本中文小說.

4. 我們在門口等你，你別在房間裡說話，快出 ___ 吧.

5. 你看！ 我們給你帶 ___ 了一些點心.

6. A: 天氣真好，我們出 ___ 走走，好嗎?

   B: 好啊，可是下午我有事兒，不能回 ___ 得太晚.

7. 我妹妹在法國，我給她寄 ___ 了五十元.

8. 他們到公園去玩的時候沒帶照相機 ___.

9. 王主任和我們在裡邊等你，請進 ___ 吧.

I. Fill in blanks with 才 or 就.

1. 我們在外邊等了很久 ___ 進來.

2. 我們在外邊等了一會兒 ___ 進來了.

3. 今天車真擠，我們在路上花了一個小時 ___ 到這兒.

4. 車 ___ 要開了，請大家上車吧.

5. 我很早 ___ 聽說過李自成的故事.

6. 《李自成》這本小說我以前沒聽說過，到今天 ___ 知道有這本書.

7. 要是我沒帶照相機，我 ___ 不能照相了.

8. 你們先進教室去，我一會兒 ___ 來.

9. 電影八點 ___ 開始，可是他們六點半 ___ 到電影院門口了.

10. 你們從東邊下山去. 他們 ___ 在山腳下.

11. 要是今天不考試，我 ___ 晚一點再去學院.

12. 秋天了. 樹葉 ___ 要紅了.

II. Insert 了 at appropriate positions in the following sentences.

1. 我的同學給我送來兩張運動會的票.

2. 你帶那本小說來嗎?

3. 學生不在這兒. 他們進教室去.

4. 他們去北海玩，帶照相機去嗎?

5. 我給我姐姐寄一本小說去.

Practical Chinese Reader #41 Exercise C

Complete the following dialogues:

1. A: 對不起, ____________________.

   B: 沒關係, ____________________.

2. A: 你怎麼現在才來?

   B: ____________________.

3. A: ____________________.

   B: 我沒帶來. 我明天給你送去.

4. A: ____________________.

   B: 我們們從西邊上山吧.

5. A: 我不送了, 請慢慢兒走.

   B: 謝謝, ____________________.

6. A: ____________________.

   B: 太好了, 你想得真周到.

7. A: ____________________.

   B: 要是明天不下雨, 我們就去參觀天安門廣場.

8. A: 今天外邊人多極了.

   B: ____________________.

9. A: 星期天你想作什麼?

   B: ____________________ 或者 ____________________.

Practical Chinese Reader #41 Exercise D

Translate into Chinese:

1. The guide is waiting for us at the entrance. Let's go out.

2. The building is in the square. Let's go over there to take a look.

3. Where are the guests? They went downstairs.

4. When will the driver return? We will go up the mountain in a while.

5. Having finished washing the clothes, he came back to the dormitory.

6. Have you brought your camera? Come over and take a picture of the pavilion.

7. I heard that he mailed twenty dollars to his younger brother.

8. I brought some snacks for you guys.

9. The doctor did not come to the infirmary.

10. We will go back home as soon as the semester ends.

Practical Chinese Reader #41 Exercise E

Translate into Chinese:

1. If the weather is nice, you can see streets and buildings of Beijing clearly.

2. If I had received my friend's telephone call, I would not have gone out.

3. I didn't know anything about the story of this Chinese emperor until I read this historical novel.

4. The driver did not come back until when we were about to set off.

5. He heard that this novel was in the store. He then went downtown to buy it.

6. A: How come you came so late?
   B: I am sorry. The bus was too crowded. It took me more than an hour to get here.
   A: Have you brought the novel that I wanted?
   B: I left it at home. Either I can send it to you tomorrow or you can pick it up at my home (go to my home to take it) today.
   A: You're very thoughtful, but I'm going back home shortly.

Resultative verbs may be used in two different modes: the actual mode and the potential mode. What we have learned previously are those in actual mode, i.e., they denotes completed or expected to be completed events. The potential mode of the resultative verbs indicates whether a subject is able to cause the result to take place after taking the action.

The potential mode is expressed in the following forms.

A. Positive: V1 + 得 + V2
 聽得懂 (be able to listen and understand)
 看得見 (be able to see)
 收得到 (be able to receive)

B. Negative: V1 + bu + V2
 看不完 (be unable to finish reading)
 修不好 (be unable to repair)
 找不到 (be unable to find)

C. Interrogative: V1 得 V2 + V1 不 V2
 作得完作不完 (be able to finish?)
 看得懂看不懂 (be able to read and understand?)

There are certain verbs which belong to V2 category and which occur in a potential mode only.

D. 了 -- to be able to
 完成得了 (be able to finish)
 用不了 (be unable to use up)
 回答不了 (be unable to answer)
 實現得了 (be able to carry out)

E. 下 -- to accommodate
 放得下 (be able to store)
 掛得下 (have the space to hang)
 坐得下 (be able to seat)

F. 動 -- to move
 跑得動 (have the energy to run)
 騎不動 (be unable to ride)
 跳不動 (be unable to jump)

Verbs with directional complements may also take potential mode.

G. 上得去 (be able to go up)
 進不來 (be unable to come in)

Practical Chinese Reader #42 Exercise A

Fill in blanks with resultative verb complements.

1. 你說得太快，我聽不 ____.
2. 汽車擠得 ____ 八個人嗎?
3. 那個書店裡買得 ____ 《李自成》嗎?
4. 這些活兒，那個退休的老工人幹得 ____ 幹不 ____?
5. 這個城太小了，看不 ____ 中國電影.
6. 你吃得 ____ 這麼多東西嗎?
7. 天氣預報說，明天會下雨，我們去得 ____ 去不 ____ 公園?
8. 這張椅子太重，你搬*不 ____ 吧.
9. 我的裙子在哪兒? 我不知道. 我找不 ____.
10. 這個廣場停得 ____ 多少車?
11. 東西這麼多，你拿得 ____ 拿不 ____?
12. 自行車太舊了，我想我修不 ____.
13. 箱子這麼小，放得 ____ 這麼多的東西嗎?
14. 他身體不好，明天參加不 ____ 運動會了.
15. 衣服太多了，我洗不 ____.
16. 天安門廣場站得 ____ 一百萬人.
17. 這些工作你完成得 ____ 完成不 ____?
18. 我還看不 ____ 中文雜誌.
19. 練習很多，你作得 ____ 嗎?
20. 你寫的字太小了，我看不 ____.

Practical Chinese Reader #42 Exercise B

I. Fill in blanks with appropriate potential resultative verbs.

1. 山上的亭子你 ________ 嗎? 太遠了，我 ________.
2. 這本小說你 ________ 嗎? 我的英文不好，我 ________.
3. 這些生詞你 ________? 生詞不多，我 ________.
4. 今天老師給的練習你 ________ ________?

   練習太難了，我 ________.
5. 在美國你們 ________ 中國菜嗎?

   美國有很多中國飯館，我們 ________ 中國菜.
6. 今天照的照片你 ________ ________?

   照片不太多，我想我 ________.
7. 那個正在修建的禮堂，明年 ________ 嗎?

   工人很多，我想 ________.
8. 箱子這麼重，你 ________ 嗎?

   這個箱子不太重，我 ________.
9. 這輛自行車你 ________ 嗎?

   沒問題，我一定 ________.
10. 桌子這麼大，你 ________ 嗎?

    我一個人 ________.
11. 這間房間 ________ 四個人嗎?

    房間太小，____________ 四個人.
12. 這些活兒，你一個人 ________ ________?

    活兒太重了，我一個人 ________.

Practical Chinese Reader #42 Exercise B

II. Fill in blanks with proper words of measurement.

1. 這個尺有多 ____?　　一米.

2. 這個房間有多 ____?　二十平方米*.

3. 這張桌子有多 ____?　三十公斤*.

4. 這位老爺爺今年多 ____ 歲數了?　他今年六十九歲.

5. 這個門有多 ____ ?　　三米.

6. 這塊布有多 ____ ?　　一尺.

III. Write out the figures in Chinese characters.

1. 6,428 ____________________

2. 9,730 ____________________

3. 5,200 ____________________

4. 20,000 ____________________

5. 45,000 ____________________

6. 91,326 ____________________

Practical Chinese Reader #42 Exercise C

Answer the following questions:

1. 天安門有多高?

2. 天安門廣場站得下多少人?

3. 廣場中間是什麼? 西邊是什麼? 東邊有什麼?

4. 人民大會堂裡邊的大禮堂有多大? 一共幾層?

5. 人民大會堂是哪年修建的? 用了多長時間完成的?

6. 人民大會堂坐得下多少人?

7. 人民大會堂是現代建築還是古代建築?

8. 典型的中國古代建築有些什麼?

9. 你們學院有多少學生?

10. 美國有多少人口(population)?

Practical Chinese Reader #42 Exercise D

Translate into Chinese:

1. The film can't be developed by evening.

2. Can you see the pavilion on the hill?

3. I was unable to find the construction site you mentioned.

4. This car can seat five people.

5. The worker was unable to do such a heavy job.

6. There are so many things. Are you able to take them?

7. A: How tall is your younger brother?
   B: He is one hundred and senventy-nine centimeters tall.

8. A: How big is this auditorium?
   B: This auditorium is forty meters wide, and fifty meters long. It can accommodate several thousand people.

9. Although he is eighty years old, he can still walk around, hear things, and see things clearly.

10. A: How come you did not go into the auditorium?
    B: There were many people in the doorway. I could not get in.

I. More about verbs and their directional complements!

Verbal phrases which have the form V1V2V3 (see #41 Grammar Notes) may take a noun phrase as object or a place word as destination.

A. Place words as destinations

Subj (+ OE) + V1 + V2 + Place + V3 + OE
他 跑 上 樓 去 了。
(He went upstairs.)

汽車 不能 開 進 公園裡 來。
(Cars are not allowed to drive into the park.)

B. When the verb of a sentence takes a direct object, there are two possibilities.

1. Subj (+ OE) + V1 + V2 + V3 + Object (+ OE)
他 給你 帶 回 來 那本小說 了。
(He has brought back that novel for you.)

2. Subj (+ OE) + V1 + V2 + Object + V3
他 每星期 寄 回 一封信 去。
(He sends a letter back every week.)

II. The coordinator 又 ... 又
(both ... and; not only ... but also)

又 ... 又 is used to connect two verbal phrases. It must connect two expressions of the same nature, i.e., they must belong to the same grammatical category.

Subj + you + SV1/VP1 + you + SV2/VP2
他心裡 又 高興 又 難過。
(He feels both happy and sad.)

今天 又 刮風 又 下雨。
(Not only is it windy, but it is also raining.)

Practical Chinese Reader #43 Exercise A

Fill in blanks with appropriate vocabulary.

1. A: 我 又 累 又 餓，我們找一 家 飯館吃飯吧.

   B: 我也有 點 兒 餓了.

2. 你看，穿 了 馬路，那兒有一 些 小吃店，我們過去看看吧!

3. 這是一家北京 風 味 的小吃店，裡邊坐著很多 雇 客.

4. 小吃店裡有 各 種小吃，都是北京風味的.

5. A: 你們二位吃 些 什麼?

   B: 來 四個油餅，兩 張 炸糕.

6. 要是不 夠，再來一碗豌豆粥，怎 麼 樣?

7. 別 ____ 中國菜我也吃過，可是我比 ____ 喜歡吃北京風味的中國菜.

8. 英國人喝茶跟中國人不一樣，他們喜歡加 ____ ____ 和 ____.

9. 這家飯館的服務員都很 ____ ____，服務也很 ____ ____. 我們走的時候，他們還請我們 ____ 意見.

10. 這是杏仁豆腐，你 ____ ____，作得好不好?

11. 你 ____ ____ 餓了嗎? 怎麼不多吃一點?

Fill in blanks with complex directional complements:

1. 禮堂門口怎麼站著這麼多的人? 我們走 ________ 看看吧!

2. 一個孩子從屋裡跑 ________, 大聲叫道: "爸爸, 你回來了."

3. "那幅畫, 掛在牆上了嗎?"

   "已經掛 ________ 了."

4. 別站著說話, 大家坐 ________ 談吧!

5. 那張桌子, 你從外邊搬 ________ 了嗎?

6. 他從箱子裡拿 ____ 兩件襯衫 ____.

7. 主席從門口走 ____ 禮堂 ____ 的時候, 我們都站了 ________.

8. 我請弟弟從郵局買 ________ 二十張郵票.

9. 那個牌子已經從門上拿 ________ 了.

10. (在飯館裡) "菜太多了, 吃不完."

    "沒關係, 吃不完我們可以帶 ________."

11. 前邊是綠燈*, 我們可以快一點開 ________.

12. 我們都不在屋裡, 你快走 ________ 吧!

13. 我昨天沒從老師那兒拿 ____ 本子 ____.

14. 寫好的信你寄 ________了沒有?

15. 我們今天可以去看京劇了. 小張昨天給我們送 ________ 兩張票.

Practical Chinese Reader #43 Exercise C

Translate into Chinese:

1. Who has walked in (here) from outside?

2. He did not run out (there).

3. The customer has walked into the restaurant.

4. The athlete swam across the river (to us).

5. Did you buy and bring some snacks back from the snack shop?

6. What did you bring back from school?

7. He did not take the camera back (here).

8. As for the letter, I've sent it out already.

9. The chef (master worker) brought out two fried cakes.

10. A: I feel both hungry and tired.
    B: Don't stand there. Sit down.

Practical Chinese Reader #43 Exercise D

Translate into Chinese:

1. He took out two shirts from the suitcase.

2. Cars are not allowed to drive into the park.

3. A: I'm a bit hungry. Let's go into the snack shop to have something.
   B: O.K.
   C: What would you like to eat?
   B: Is there a menu*?
   C: Yes. Here it is.
   A: This restaurant has all kinds of Beijing style snacks.
   B: Give us two deep-fried pancakes and two bowls of almond junket.
   C: Anything else?
   A: No. Your service is superb.
   C: It's our duty.

Practical Chinese Reader #43 Exercise E

Write a short script describing a scene in a Chinese restaurant.

Suggested vocabulary: 服務員，顧客，菜單*，餓，渴*，汽水，好吃，

別的，風味.

I. 是 ... 的 as a focus marker

是 may be placed before an element with 的 usually occurring at the end of a sentence to express that the element is the focus of the sentence where it occurs. The element can be a subject, a place word, a time expression, a prepositional phrase indicating manner, or a verb phrase. The construction is used with the presupposition that an event has taken place and the speaker intends to know or to give more information about it.

A. Subj + 是 + Time + Predicate + 的

	Subj	是	Time	Predicate	的
X.	我母親			到中國去了。	
	(My mother went to China.)				
Y.	她	是	什麼時候	去	的?
	(WHEN did she go?)				
X.	她	是	上星期	去	的。
	(She went last week.)				

B. 他是從上海來的。
(It was from Shanghai that he came.)

我們是坐飛機去的。
(It was by air that we went.)

他們不是來工作的。
(They did not come to work.)

是張老師給我們介紹頤和園的。
(It was Prof. Zhang who told us about the Summer Palace.)

Note: When a verb takes an object, 的 may occur either inbetween the verb and its object or at the end of a sentence. For example:

他是甚麼時候去的廣州?

他是甚麼時候去廣州的?

II. Sentences with subject-verb reversion are those where expressions of location are more emphasized.

Location + VP + NP
他家 來了 幾位客人。
(There were several guests at his house.)

從車裡 走下來 幾個人。
(There came several people from the car.)

III. Exclamatory sentences are expressed by 多(麼) ... 啊, or by 太 ... 了。

Subj + duo(mo)/tai + SV + Particle
那位服務員 多 熱情 啊!
(How nice that clerk is!)

這兒的風景 多麼 美 啊!
(How beautiful the scenery is!)

太 好 了!
(That is terrific!)

IV. 只有 ... 才 (only when ... then) connects two sentences. Both 只有 and 才 are placed before a verb if the subjects of the sentences in question are identical. 只有 occurs at the beginning of the first sentence if the two subjects have different referents.

A. Subj + zhiyou + Predicate1 (+ Subj) + cai + Predicate2
你 只有 自己去看看, (你) 才 能了解那兒的情況。
(Only when you take a look yourself can you understand the condition there.)

B. zhiyou + Subj1 + Predicate1 + Subj2 + cai + Predicate2
只有 他 來, 我們 才 能去。
(Only when he comes can we go.)

V. SV + 得 + VP (so SV that ... VP)

他難過得哭了起來。
(He was so sad that he started to cry.)

她累得不能走路。
(She was so tired that she could not walk at all.)

Practical Chinese Reader #44 Exercise A

Fill in blanks with appropriate vocabulary.

1. 秋天來了，葉子都紅了. 外邊的 ____ ____ 很美，像一 ____ 畫兒一樣.

2. 春天的時候，地上的綠 ____ 都長出來了.

3. ____ 山是一種很好的運動.

4. ____ ____ 每天從東邊出來，從西邊下去.

5. 這幾年中國和美國的 ____ ____ 很多.

6. 昆明湖後邊是一 ____ 山，叫萬壽山.

7. 我們的中文一天 ____ 一天進步.

8. A: 明天你們去頤和園玩，我作你們的嚮導.

   B: 太好 ____!

9. 你看！這兒的風景多麼美 ____!

10. 明年夏天我決定到中國去 ____ 行.

11. A: 你常常出去看電影嗎?

    B: 不，只有星期六晚上我 ____ 出去看電影.

12. 他們不 ____ 來度假*的，他們 ____ 來談貿易的.

13. 他聽了以後高興得跳 ____ ____.

14. 頤和園是有名的古典 ____ ____.

15. 冬天來了. 天氣一天比 ____ ____ 冷了.

Practical Chinese Reader #44 Exercise B

Following sentences are possible answers to certain questions. Give an appropriate quertion form to each of them.

1. 我是上星期去的頤和園.

2. 我弟弟是一九七五年生的.

3. 他們是坐飛機從廣州到北京的.

4. 他是跟兩個同學一起到昆明旅行的.

5. 他們這次是來參觀工廠的.

6. 我不是從公園去的. 我是從飯館去的.

7. 草地上坐著幾個年輕人.

8. 你只有自己去看看, 才能了解到那兒的情況.

9. 我不是騎車來的.

10. 湖邊有一個亭子.

Practical Chinese Reader #44 Exercise C

Answer questions on the basis of the text:

1. 頤和園是哪一年開始修建的?

2. 萬壽山爲什麼叫這個名字?

3. 萬壽山上有什麼?

4. 頤和園裡的長廊有多長?

5. 長廊上邊有什麼?

6. 哪兒有一個白塔?

7. 古波説的山上的畫兒是什麼?

8. 你看過《三國演義》嗎? 那是一本什麼樣的小説?

9. 昆明湖在哪兒?

Practical Chinese Reader #44 Exercise D

Translate into Chinese:

1. It was last week that her mother came.

2. It was with a tourist group that they traveled.

3. When was it that he decided to come with the trade delegation?

4. It was by boat that they went to Japan.

5. The car came from behind.

6. From the lakeside, an old man walked toward us here.

7. From the car, several people walked out.

8. How cordial the sales clerk is!

9. How beautiful the scenery here is!

Practical Chinese Reader #44 Exercise E

Translate into Chinese:

1. Nobody knows how much he likes Chinese paintings.

2. Only when the sun is out is Kunming Lake as bright as a mirror.

3. Only when you speak more, listen more, and read more can you learn a foreign language well.

4. Only when you walk to the lakeside can you see the bridge.

5. He was so sad that he began to cry.

6. She was so happy that she shouted loudly: "That's great!"

7. I feel that Chinese is becoming more interesting everyday.

8. The quality of this type of chinaware has been improved year by year.

Practical Chinese Reader #45 Exercise A

Fill in blanks with 的，地 or 得.

1. 熊貓吃 ____ 是竹葉. 他們在竹林裡不停 ____ 走來走去.

2. 觀眾看見了可愛 ____ 熊貓都熱烈 ____ 鼓掌.

3. 從山上 ____ 公園看過去，山下 ____ 建築看 ____ 清清楚楚.

4. 見到了從國外回來 ____ 朋友，他高興 ____ 跳了起來.

5. 這兒 ____ 風景真美! 青 ____ 山，綠 ____ 水，遠遠 ____ 山上還有一個亭子.

6. 每個學生都認真 ____ 在圖書館裡學習.

7. 孩子們高高興興 ____ 到學校去了.

8. 她女兒有一雙大大 ____ 眼睛，非常像她媽媽.

9. 今天照 ____ 照片洗 ____ 好嗎?

10. 他們不是來工作 ____，他們是來旅行 ____.

11. 熊貓 ____ 樣子又可愛又可笑. 肥肥 ____ 身體，短短 ____ 腿，眼睛上像戴著墨鏡.

12. 雪下 ____ 這麼大，我們出 ____ 去嗎?

Practical Chinese Reader #45 Exercise B

Fill in blanks with 才 or 就.

1. 車 ____ 要開了，請大家坐好.

2. ____ 他一個人來，別人都出去玩兒了.

3. 只有作完功課以後，我們 ____ 能出去看電影.

4. 我 ____ 有一件綠襯衫.

5. 我找了半個多小時 ____ 找到你家.

6. 他昨天跳舞跳得太晚了. 今天上午十點鐘 ____ 起床.

7. 他三歲的時候 ____ 跟母親到外國去了.

8. 要是明天是晴天，我們 ____ 到頤和園去玩兒.

9. 昨天上午我們沒回宿舍，到晚上吃完了飯以後我們 ____ 回去.

10. 昨天吃了晚飯以後，我們 ____ 去聽音樂了.

11. 你從這兒往西走，過兩個路口，____ 可以看見那個小吃店了.

12. 我們又累又餓，在小吃店裡吃了四個油餅，六塊炸糕，兩碗豆腐湯 ____ 回家.

Practical Chinese Reader #45 Exercise C

Give negative forms for the following sentences:

1. 他說漢語說得很流利.

2. 這個工廠的工人工作得跟那個工廠的工人一樣認真.

3. 我昨天從箱子裡找出一條裙子來.

4. 在那個書店裡買得到這本英文小說.

5. 我在動物園看過兩次熊貓.

6. 熊貓的樣子比別的動物可愛.

7. 他們是跟貿易團到廣州來的.

8. 從非洲來的學生跟從南亞來的一樣多.

9. 那個禮堂坐得下五千人.

10. 我們作完了練習才去看電影.

11. 那張桌子兩個人搬得動.

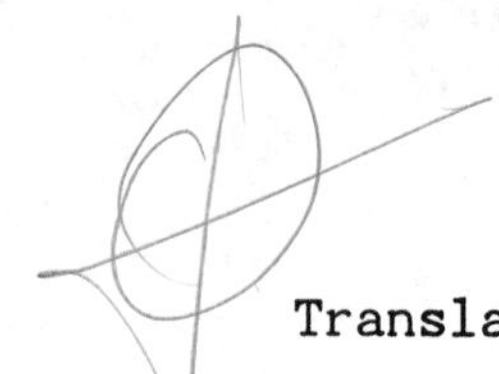

Practical Chinese Reader #45 Exercise D

Translate into Chinese:

1. A: Did you hear what the chairman said?
   B: No, the platform is too far away. I was unable to hear clearly.

2. There were so many people in the zoo. We could not get in.

3. A: How big is the table?
   B: It's five feet long, three feet wide.

4. The look of a panda is both lovely and funny.

5. As soon as she saw her daughter, she was so excited that she began to cry.

6. I've brought a tour guide for you.

7. If your sister does not come and take the camera, we will then mail it to her.

8. That novel was written ten years ago. He has not written any book since then.

把-Construction

A sentence with Ba-construction emphasizes how an object of a sentence is disposed or handled. In a 把-sentence the object of a verb is preposed to the position before the verb and after 把 to form a prepositional phrase. For example:

Subject	(+Adv/Neg)	+ Ba	+ Object	+ Verb	+ Aspect/Complement	
他		把	衣服	洗	乾淨了。	
(He washed the clothes.)						
你		把	錄音機	帶	來了	嗎?
(Did you bring the tape-recorder?)						
(請)你		把	窗户	開	開。	
(Please open the window.)						
我		把	這件事兒	忘	了。	
(I forgot this matter.)						
你		把	名字	寫	一寫。	
(Write your name.)						
他	沒	把	信	寫	得很好。	
(He did not write the letter well.)						
我	明天	把	照相機	帶	來。	
(I will bring the camera tomorrow.)						
嚮導		把	那個學生	帶	來了。	
(The guide has brougnt the student here.)						

There are several noticeable features about a Ba-sentence:

1. The verb must be an action verb. Verbs such as 喜歡, 有, 是, 知道, etc. can not occur in a Ba-structure.

2. The object must be a definite noun, i.e., it must have a referent.

3. The verb connot stand alone, i.e., the verb must be followed by other element(s). The element(s) may simply be an aspect marker 了 or 著, or a directional complemnent, a quantitative verb modifier, a degree adverbial, or a resultative complement.

4. Negation 不/沒有 is placed before the preposition 把. Other expressions such as time expressions or modals also occur before the preposition.

Practical Chinese Reader #46 Exercise A

Fill in blanks with appropriate vocabulary.

I. 帕蘭卡昨天晚上睡覺的時候沒把窗户 ____ 上，今天可能感 ____ 了。她覺得很不 ____ ____ ，頭 ____ ，咳 ____ ，又發 ____ ，病得很厲 ____。

她到 ____ ____ 去看大夫。大夫給她 ____ 了體溫，說是重感冒，要 ____ 院。聽了大夫的話，她 ____ ____ 辦住院手續，在病房裡躺了一天，____ 了藥，____ 了針以後，已經 ____ 多了。

II. 1. 請把門開 ____ 。

2. 我已經把電視關 ____ 了。

3. 你把我帶來的錄音聽一 ____ 吧。

4. 你把餃子包 ____ 了嗎?

5. 請他把帶去的東西檢查 ____ ____ 。

6. 請護士* 把病人的體溫量一 ____ 。

7. 你把花兒都種 ____ 了沒有?

8. 媽媽把衣服都洗 ____ 了。

9. 你把藥吃 ____ 沒有?

10. 他沒把我的照相機帶 ____ 。

Practical Chinese Reader #46 Exercise B

Change the following sentences into sentences with 把-construction.

1. 請你立刻開開錄音機，我想聽聽。

2. 昨天晚上我沒關上窗户，所以感冒了。

3. 這件事兒，他們告訴了我。

4. 大夫請護士* 量一量他的體温。

5. 姥姥包好了餃子，大家就開始吃了。

6. 錄音機錄上了他説的話。

7. 他忘了吃藥了，所以病沒好。

他忘了把藥吃了，所以病沒好。

8. 那張照片你還給了他沒有?

9. 請拿出掛號證* 來。

10. 葡萄他沒洗乾淨。

他沒把葡萄乾淨

Practical Chinese Reader #46 Exercise C

Answer questions with 把-construction.

1. 我的錄音機怎麼不見了?

2. 他送來的葡萄在哪兒?

3. 病房裡爲什麼這麼冷?

4. 電視機還開著嗎?

5. 你給你朋友寄去了什麼?

6. 大夫對你作了些什麼?

7. 我的衣服在哪兒?

8. 我要帶走的東西怎麼了?

9. 我們什麼時候可以吃餃子?

Practical Chinese Reader #46 Exercise D

I. Translate into Chinese:

Doctor: What's wrong with you?

Patient: I have a headache, and a cough too. It's very likely that I have a cold.

Doctor: Let me take your temperature. Open your mouth.

Patient: Do I have a fever?

Doctor: Yes, but not too serious. How long have you had the discomfort?

Patient: Last evening.

Doctor: You have a cold. You will feel better after taking some medicine. here's the prescription.

Patient: How should I take the medicine?

Doctor: Four times a day, two tablets each time.

Patient: Thank you.

II. Controlled composition.

Write a paragraph in Chinese about your experience of seeing a doctor. You thought you caught a cold and explained to your doctor what happened. The doctor did the routine check-up on you. You did not get better after having taken the medicine prescribed by the doctor. However, you finally got better because of some other measures.

(You finish the story.)

I. 把-construction

把-construction must be employed in cases where resultative verbs or verbs with post-verbal prepositions take definite nouns as their objects.

A. Verbs with post-verbal prepositional phrases

在 -- at, in, on

他把筆忘在家裡了。	(He left his pen at home.)
你把書放在哪兒了？	(Where did you put the book?)

到 -- to

我把椅子拿到樓上去了。	(I took the chair upstairs.)
他們把我送到車站。	(They saw me to the station.)

給 -- to
我把錢交給了售票員。
(I gave the money to the ticket seller.)
請把書留給他。
(Please leave the book to him.)

B. Verbs with resultative complements

成 -- into; for
他想把房子修建成那個樣子。
(He intends to build the house like that.)
我把他看成了中國人。
(I took him for a Chinese.)

作 -- as
他們把他看作家裡人。
(They consider him as a family member.)
上海人把 "喝茶" 叫作 "吃茶"。
(People in Shanghai refer to "喝茶" as "吃茶".)

II. 除了 ... (以外) ... 還 (in addition to)
除了 ... (以外) ... 都 (except)

A. 昨天下午除了游泳，他還釣魚了。
(Yesterday afternoon he fished in addition to swimming.)

B. 除了他騎自行車去以外，我們都坐車去了。
(We all went by car but he rode a bicycle.)

Practical Chinese Reader #47 Exercise A

Fill in blanks with suitable vocabulary:

1. 魯迅的故居的院子裡有兩 ____ 棗樹.

2. 這 ____ 房子有三 ____ 臥室.

3. 我看過一 ____ 魯迅寫的文章, 也看過他寫的一 ____ 小說.

4. 美國詩人 Emily Dickinson 的 ____ ____ 在麻州安城.

5. 去年我到中國去了. 回來以後, 我很 ____ ____ 在中國的生活.

6. 參觀了有名的人的故居以後, 很多人把 ____ ____ 寫在留言簿上.

7. 除了他們倆 ____ ____, 別的人 ____ 喜歡爬山.

8. 房子的北邊 ____ 著另一個房子.

9. 這句話我看不懂, 請你給我 ____ ____ 一下.

10. ____ ____ 歷史以外, 我 ____ 喜歡藝術.

11. 魯迅給中國人民留下了 ____ ____ 的文化遺產.

Practical Chinese Reader #47 Exercise B

Fill in blanks with 成，作，在，到，or 給.

1. 北京人把 ice-lolly 叫 ____ 冰棍兒.

2. 老師把這個偉大的文學家的生活介紹 ____ 我們.

3. 我們把兩株樹種 ____ 院子裡.

4. 對不起，我忘了把書帶 ____ 學校裡來，我把書留 ____ 家裡了.

5. 我把他給我的照片留 ____ 紀念*.

6. 父母都想把孩子培養 ____ 好青年.

7. 請把句子翻譯 ____ 中文.

8. 大家把他選 ____ 主席.

9. 他們把車開 ____ 飛機場去接他.

10. 我已經把練習交 ____ 老師了.

11. 這個設計師（designer）把禮堂設計 ____ 現在這個樣子.

12. 請你把這件行李帶 ____ 我哥哥請他寄 ____ 中國去.

13. 那個老人把這個年輕人看 ____ 自己的兒子.

14. 他父親的遺產都留 ____ 了他.

15. 他把‘大夫’念 ____ 了‘dafu’.

Practical Chinese Reader #47 Exercise C

Make sentences:

1. 把 ... 看作

我把我的老師看作我的朋友。

I view my professor as my friend.

2. 把 ... 作成

3. 把 ... 留給

4. 把 ... 拿到

5. 把 ... 叫作

6. 除了 ... 以外 ... 也

7. 除了 ... 以外 ... 都

8. 除了 ... 以外 ... 還

Practical Chinese Reader #47 Exercise D

Translate into Chinese:

1. They wrote their names in the visitor's book.

2. I have already returned the book to the library.

3. They spent ten years developing the small clinic into a hospital.

3/31/99

4. They did not say "good-bye" to me until they saw me off at the station.

5. My classmates asked me to bring the tape-recorder to you.

6. They elected this worker to be director of the factory.

7. Everyone got the flu except him.

8. Besides this article, what other writings of Lu Xun's have you read?

9. The weather here is pretty good except (the fact that) it is a bit cold in winter.

10. The guide led the visitors to the courtyard.

Practical Chinese Reader #48 Grammar Notes

Interrogative pronouns (IP) which have general denotations

A. As subjects

IP	+	都/也	(+ Neg)	+ Predicate
誰		都	不	想睡覺。

(Nobody would like to sleep.)

什麼	都		好。

(Anything is good.)

哪兒	都		有人。

(There are people everywhere.)

B. As objects

Subject	+ IP	+	都/也	(+ Neg)	+	Predicate
他	什麼		都			想試一試。

(He would like to try anything.)

這位作家	哪個國家	都		去過。

(This writer has been to every country.)

Fill in blanks with vocabulary:

1. 中國的春節就 ____ 聖誕節一樣，是 ____ 家人團聚的 ____ ____.

2. 春節的時候見到別人要給人 ____ 年.

3. 在春節的時候，常常可以看到 "恭 ____ 新 ____" 這四個字.

4. 新年的時候，全家人在一起 ____ 年. 孩子們都 ____ 新衣服，新鞋，____ 新帽子，在外邊 ____ 爆竹，____ 燈籠，高興 ____ 了.

5. 中國新年是 ____*曆正月 ____ ____.

6. 春節的前一晚叫作 ____ ____*.

7. 吃年夜飯*是中國人的 ____ ____.

8. 春節的時候，很多人在門上 ____ 春聯，在牆上 ____ 年畫兒.

9. 吃年夜飯的時候，桌上總是 ____ 著很多菜.

10. 我真 ____ 想 ____ 他寫字寫得這麼整齊.

11. A: 您要的東西我都帶來了.

    B: 謝謝您，真太 ____ ____ 您了.

12. 他家裡總是 ____ 掃得很 ____ 淨.

13. A: 他 ____ ____ ____ 沒有回家?

    B: ____ ____ 最近比較忙，所以沒有回家.

Practical Chinese Reader #48 Exercise B

Complete the following sentences by supplying verbal phrases and make them sentences with a passive meaning.

1. 過年的飯菜

2. 這篇文章

3. 我買來的花兒

4. 客人的房間

5. 他帶來的新年禮物

6. 桌上的東西

7. 你朋友要的春聯

8. 孩子們的爆竹

9. 郵票都

Practical Chinese Reader #48 Exercise C

Complete the following sentences with the given interrogative pronouns.

1. 全班除了這個學生以外，________________________ （誰）

2. 除了魚以外，________________________ （什麼菜）

3. 明天我全天都有空兒 ________________________ （什麼時候）

4. 我的車壞了，還沒修好，所以 ________________________ （哪兒）

5. 菜已經作好了，但是 ________________________ （誰）

6. 練習太多了，________________________ （怎麼）

7. 昨天我去百貨大樓買東西，可是人太多了，所以 ____________

____ （什麼）

8. 你知道誰想要這件禮物？________________________ （誰）

9. 誰想去中國參觀？________________________ （哪個作家）

10. 春節的時候哪兒可以看到年畫兒？________________________ （哪兒）

Practical Chinese Reader #48 Exercise D

Answer the following questions:

1. 春聯最常貼在哪兒?

2. 春聯都是用什麼紙寫的?

3. 在美國，新年的時候放爆竹嗎?

4. 春節爲什麼要放爆竹?

5. 爲什麼中國人吃年夜飯的時候要吃魚?

6. 今年聖誕節你和誰一起過的?

7. 今年新年你過得怎麼樣?

8. 你看過中國年畫兒嗎?

Practical Chinese Reader #48 Exercise E

Translate into Chinese:

1. The room has not been cleaned up yet.

2. The lantern with the characters "Happy New Year" written on it has been hung up.

3. All the food for the New Year have been prepared.

4. Pandas are lovely animals. Everyone likes them.

5. I did not realize that he ate nothing but American food.

6. He will read books by any writer, since he loves reading.

7. I heard that people here eat dumplings at New Year, but you may have them any day.

8. We came late today because we went to bed a bit late last night.

9. I did not buy that lamp, because I did not bring enough money with me.

10. Since this winter is relatively mild, I spent my Christmas at home.

Practical Chinese Reader #49 Grammar Notes

I. Sentences of passive voice

Recipient + Neg + Prep + Actor + Verb + OE
我的自行車 讓 他 騎 走了。
(My bicycle was ridden away by him.)

我們 都 被 這個作品 感動 了。
(We were all moved by this literary work.)

我的紙 沒 叫 風 刮 走。
(My paper was not blown away by the wind.)

照相機 被 他們 拿 走了嗎?
(Was the camera taken away by them?)

II. The connective 不但 ... 而且 connects either two predicates or two sentences. Its position of occurrence varies.

A. Subject + 不但 + Predicate1 + 而且 + Predicate2
這個話劇 不但 寫得好, 而且 演得也很好。
(This play was not only well written but well performed.)

B. 不但 + Subj1 + Predicate1 + 而且 + Subj2 + Predicate2
不但 中國人 懷念他 而且 外國人 也懷念他。
(Not only did the Chinese miss him, but foreigners missed him too.)

III. 連 ... 也/都 (even) may apply to

A. a subject

連 + Subject + 都/也 + Predicate
連 孩子們 都 被吸引住了。
(Even the children were enchanted.)

連 這位作家 也 來了。
(Even this writer has come.)

B. an object

Subj + 連 + Obj + 都/也 + Predicate
他 連 衣服 也 沒有換。
(He did not even change his clothes.)

她 連 椅子 都 帶來了。
(She even brought the chair with her.)

Practical Chinese Reader #49 Exercise A

Fill in blanks with appropriate vocabulary.

1. ____ ____ 是記一個人一天的事或者感想.

2. 這個話劇要在那個很大的 ____ ____ 演出.

3. 那個話劇的 ____ ____ 非常成功.

4. 作家，畫家，演員*都是 ____ ____ 家.

5. 《茶館》是老舍寫的有名的 ____ ____ 之一.

6. 他的小説我以前看過，但是看他的話劇這 ____ 是第一次.

7. 請你給我正 ____ 的回答.

8. 中國的舊社會是一個黑 ____ 的社會.

9. 我們不但被這個話劇吸 ____ 住了，____ ____ 被它 ____ 動了.

10. 在舊社會，很多中國人民 ____ 抓，____ 殺. 有的還 ____ 逼得賣兒賣女.

11. 我 ____ ____ 喜歡聽女高音*獨唱*，而且喜歡聽民樂*.

12. 那個 ____ 人作了很多 ____事 ，所以被抓了.

13. 他連衣服 ____ 沒換就出去了.

Practical Chinese Reader #49 Exercise B

Change into passive voice:

1. 這個劇感動了勞動人民.

2. 大家把老舍叫作 "人民藝術家".

3. 小張把我的照相機借走了.

4. 這個演員成功的演出把我們都吸引住了.

5. 這個作家還沒把他的話劇翻譯成法文.

6. 在那個時代，有人不但把愛國青年抓了，而且還殺了.

7. 他不但把我的自行車借走了，而且把我的汽車也開走了.

8. 壞人連孩子也殺了.

9. 風把報紙都刮走了.

10. 除了小王以外，我誰都請了.

Practical Chinese Reader #49 Exercise C

Change the sentences into 連...也 construction with the underlined phrases as the focus of the structures. For example:

我沒有喝茶就走了.
我連茶也沒有喝就走了.

1. 那個壞人被這個話劇感動了.

2. 那個壞作品讓人借走了.

3. 我把我爸爸給我的十元錢化了.

4. 沒有錢的人不但沒有吃的，穿的，而且被逼得把兒女賣了.

5. 他沒吃完飯就走了.

Complete the following sentences:

1. 不但中國人過年的時候要團聚，而且 ______________.

2. 這兒的冬天不但雪下得很多，而且 ______________.

3. 我不但把功課作完了，而且連 ______________.

4. 那個音樂會不但有合唱*，獨唱*，而且 ______________.

5. 他不常看話劇，連 ______________.

Practical Chinese Reader #49 Exercise D

Translate into Chinese:

1. Lao She was one of the most famous writers in China.

2. What this writer wrote about was conditions in the Old Society.

3. The synopsis of this play has yet been translated into English.

4. The audience was enchanted by the language of the play.

5. Not only were the patriots arrested and killed, but the poor were forced to work.

6. This novel not only enhanced my knowledge of the Chinese history but also deepened my understanding of the Chinese people.

7. We not only read his works but also translated them into other languages.

8. Even the actor was moved by his own successful performance.

9. The delegation stayed in Beijing for a short time. They did not even visit Yi-He-Yuan (the Summer Palace).

10. Not only have the students not been to a tea house, but not even their teacher has been to one.

Practical Chinese Reader #50 Exercise A

Fill in blanks with appropriate vocabulary.

1. 這位有名的作家的作品，有的我看過，____ ____ 我沒看過.
2. 今年我是在中國過 ____ 春節.
3. 這家飯館的小吃，____ 好吃又便宜.
4. ____ ____ 外邊天氣太冷了，所以我們昨晚沒出去.
5. ____ ____ 這位偉大的藝術家逝世了，但是大家還是懷念著他.
6. 青年們都 ____ 魯迅看作自己的好朋友，好老師.
7. 我一看見她 ____ 覺得她像我的姐姐.
8. 你要是今天不太忙，____ 請到我家來坐坐.
9. 只有不太忙的時候我 ____ 能到外邊走走.
10. 除了游泳 ____ ____，他們 ____ 釣魚了.
11. 誰 ____ 大家叫作 "人民藝術家"?
12. 這位藝術家 ____ ____ 在中國很有名，而且在世界上也很有名.
13. 誰 ____ 會被這兒的風景吸引住.
14. ____ ____ 風雪很大，但是梅花還是挺立著.
15. 太熱了，請你 ____ 窗户打開.
16. 我們都去參觀那個畫展了，連老師 ____ 去了.
17. 這個學生不很聰明，____ 不用功.
18. 他每天 ____ 到十二點就睡覺了.
19. ____ ____ 每天練習說漢語，漢語才能說得很流利.
20. ____ ____ 每天練習說漢語，漢語就能說得很流利.

Practical Chinese Reader #50 Exercise B

Complete the following sentences:

1. 花兒被

2. 我把錢

3. 他們是上星期六

4. 禮堂裡邊

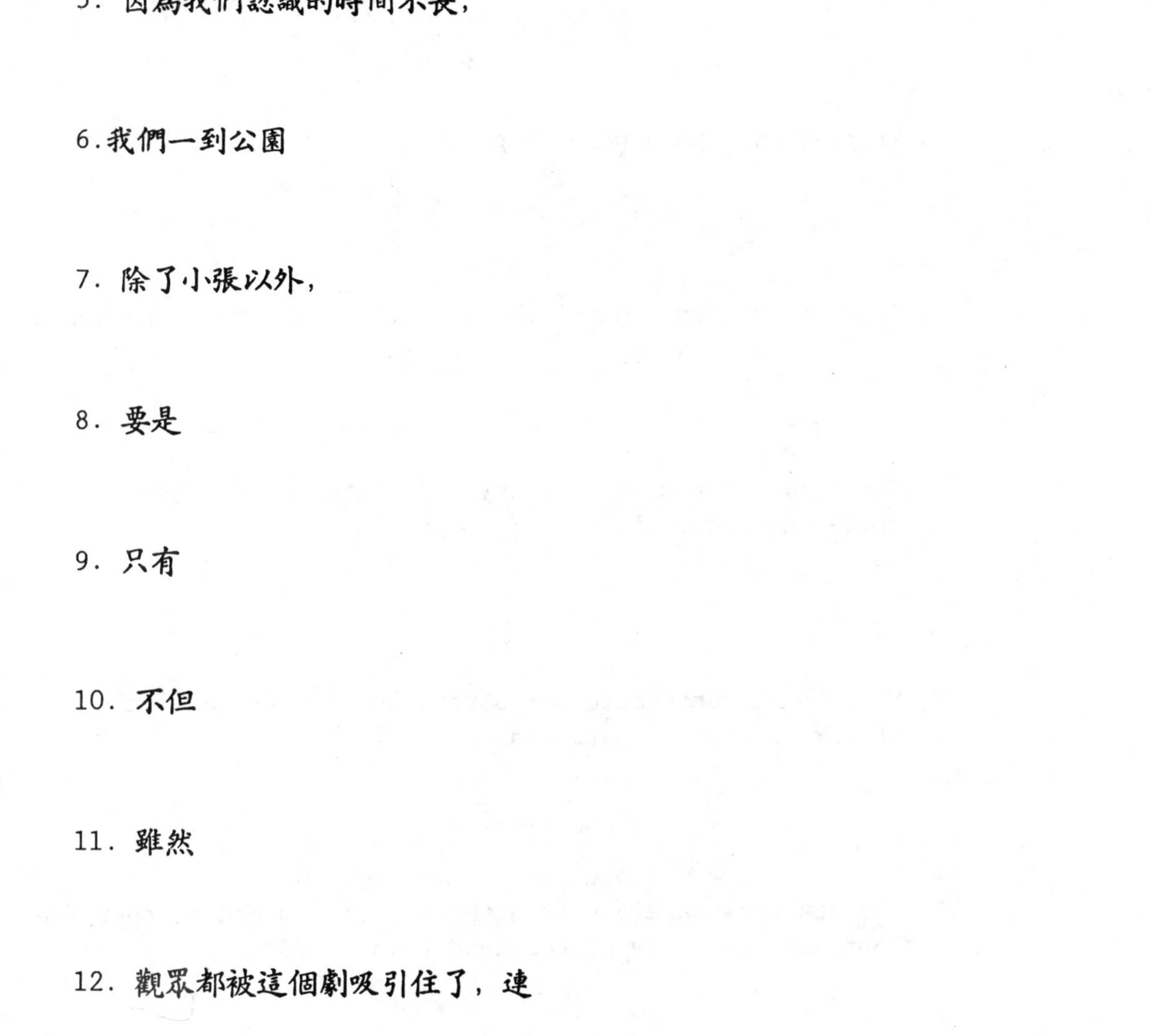

5. 因爲我們認識的時間不長,

6.我們一到公園

7. 除了小張以外,

8. 要是

9. 只有

10. 不但

11. 雖然

12. 觀眾都被這個劇吸引住了, 連

Practical Chinese Reader #50 Exercise C

Translate into Chinese:

1. It was in 1976 that the premier passed away.

2. Only when one writes characters stroke by stroke can one write them beautifully.

3. Last Sunday was their twentieth wedding anniversary.

4. We read his diary page by page.

5. This painter was one of the greatest artists in the world.

6. The guide at the art gallery said with smile, "Your comments, please."

7. The one who attracted our attention most was a little girl of six or seven (years old).

8. The students came out from the auditorium one by one. The last one was a boy of thirteen (years old).

Appendix I

Character	Pinyin	English	Lesson
		a	
阿姨	āyí	auntie	39
愛	ài	to love	45
		b	
把	bǎ	a preposition	46
把	bǎ	a measure word	47
百	bǎi	hundred	33
擺	bǎi	to put; to lay (the table)	48
百貨大樓	Bǎihuò Dàlóu	The (Beijing) Department Store	36
拜年	bàinián	pay a New Year call; wish somebody a happy New Year	48
搬	bān	to move; to take away	42
班	bān	class; squad	42
辦公室	bàngōngshì	office	42
包	bāo	to wrap; to make (dumplings)	48
包裹	bāoguǒ	parcel	39
薄	báo	thin	34
保持	bǎochí	to keep/retain	40
爆竹	bàozhú	firecracker	48
北邊	běibián	north; northern part	47
北海	Běihǎi	Beihai Park	32
北京動物園	Běijīng Dòngwùyuán	the Beijing Zoo	45
北京語言學院	Běijīng YǔYán Xuéyuàn	Beijing Languages Institute	31
被	bèi	a preposition	49
本	běn	this; one's own; native	34
本子	běnzi	book; notebook	39
逼	bī	to force; to compel	32
鼻子	bízi	nose	32
筆	bǐ	a measure word	50
比較	bǐjiào	comparatively; quite; to compare	43
畢業	bìyè	to graduate	44
邊	biān	side; edge (of a lake, etc.)	44

遍	biàn	a measure word	32
表	biǎo	form （telegraph forms, etc.）	32
表	biǎo	（wrist） watch	35
别的	biéde	other; another	43
别人	biérén	other people; others	36
冰棍兒	bīnggùnr	ice-lolly; ice-sucker	42
病	bìng	to be ill; illness	32
病房	bìngfáng	ward （of a hospital）	46
病人	bìngrén	patient	46
不但…而且…	búdàn…érqiě…	not only … but also …	49
布	bù	cotton cloth	34
不好意思	bù hǎoyìsi	to feel embarrassed; to feel embarrassing （to do something）	39
布鞋	bùxié	cloth shoes	37
不用	búyòng	there is no need to	31

c/ch

才	cái	only; just; not…until	41
彩旗	cáiqí	colored flag	40
菜單	càidān	menu	43
操場	cāochǎng	sportsground	40
草	cǎo	grass	44
茶館	cháguǎn	teahouse	49
茶壺	cháhú	teapot	36
茶具	chájù	tea set; tea service	36
茶碗	cháwǎn	teacup	36
長	cháng	long	31
長城	Chángchēng	The Great Wall	32
長廊	Cháng Láng	Long Corridor	44
長短	chángduǎn	length	37
車間	chējiān	workshop	39
陳毅	Chén Yì	Chen Yi	33
成	chéng	to become; to turn into	47
成功	chénggōng	to succeed	49
成績	chéngjī	result; achievement	35
尺	chǐ	ruler	42
崇禎	Chóngzhēn	Emperor Chongzhen	41
綢子	chóuzi	silk fabric	37
出	chū	to come out; to go out	31
初	chū	a prefix	48

出差	chūchái	to be away on official business; be on a business trip	44
出院	chūyuàn	to leave hospital	47
出租汽車	chūzūqìchē	taxi; cab	38
除了...以外	chúle...yǐwài	besides; except	47
除夕	chúxī	New Year's Eve	48
穿（馬路）	chuān（mǎlù）	to cross （a street）	43
船	chuán	boat	44
窗户	chuānghu	window	44
窗口	chuāngkǒu	window	34
春節	chūnjié	Spring Festival	48
春聯	chūnlián	Spring Festival couplets; New Year scrolls	48
春天	chūntián	spring	39
瓷器	cíqì	chinaware; porcelain	36
次	cì	a measure word; time	31
聰明	cōngming	intelligent; bright	39
存車處	cúnchēchù	parking lot （for bicycles）	43
錯	cuò	wrong	38
錯誤	cuòwù	mistake	47

d

達尼亞	Dáníyà	name of a person	44
打（拳）	dǎ（quán）	to do shadowboxing	40
打（針）	dǎ（zhēn）	to give/have an injection	46
打開	dǎkāi	to open	50
打破	dǎpò	to break	40
打掃	dǎsǎo	to clean up	48
大便	dàbiàn	stool; human excrement	46
大鬧天宮	Dànàotiāngōng	"The Monkey Creates Havoc in Heaven"	32
大娘	dàniáng	aunt	38
大聲	dàshēng	in loud voice; loudly	34
大學	dàxué	university; college	31
大爺	dàye	uncle	38
帶	dài	to take （along）; to bring （with）	38
戴	dài	to wear （e.g. cap, glasses, gloves）	45
袋	dài	bag; sack	48
單	dān	bill; list; form	34
但是	dànshì	but	39
當心	dāngxīn	to take care; to look out	43
得（病）	dé（bìng）	to fall ill; to contract a disease	32

地	de	a structural particle	34
燈	dēng	lantern; lamp; light	48
燈節	dēngjié	the Lantern Festival (15th of the 1st month of the lunar calendar)	48
燈籠	dēnglong	lantern	48
第	dì	a prefix indicating order	31
地方	dìfang	place	32
地鐵	dìtié	the underground; subway	38
典型	diǎnxíng	typical; model	42
店	diàn	shop; store	43
電報	diànbào	telegram; cable	34
電車	diànchē	trolleybus	38
吊	diào	to hang	41
訂	dìng	to subscribe to (a newspaper, etc.)	36
定作	dìngzuò	to have something made; to order	37
丟	diū	to lose	41
東邊	dōngbiān	east; eastern part	38
東西	dōngxi	thing	30
動	dòng	to move	42
動物	dòngwù	animal	45
動物園	dòngwùyuán	zoo	45
豆腐	dòufu	bean curd	43
獨唱	dúchàng	solo; to solo	43
度	dù	a measure word, degree	33
度假	dùjià	to spend one's holidays	44
短	duǎn	short	37
對	duì	to; for	39
對不起	duìbuqǐ	(I'm) sorry	41
對象	duìxiàng	boy or girl friend	44
多麼	duōme	how; what	44

e

餓	è	to be hungry; hungry	43
兒子	érzi	son	48
耳朵	ěrduo	ear	32

f

發燒	fāshāo	to have a fever	46
發展	fāzhǎn	to develop	36

飯館	fànguǎn	restaurant	43
方便	fāngbiàn	convenient; to make it convenient for	42
方向	fāngxiàng	direction	38
放	fàng	to put; to place	34
放（爆竹）	fàng（bàozhú）	to let off （firecrackers）	48
放（假）	fàng（jià）	to have a holiday or vacation	35
非洲	Fēizhōu	Africa	45
肥	féi	loose-fitting; fat	37
肺	fèi	lungs	32
肺炎	fèiyán	pneumonia	32
分	fēn	a measure word （the smallest Chinese monetary unit）	36
風	fēng	wind	33
封	fēng	a measure word	34
豐富	fēngfù	rich; abundant; to enrich	47
風景	fēngjǐng	scenery; landscape	44
風俗	fēngsú	custom	48
風味	fēngwèi	local flavor; local style	43
服務	fúwù	service; to serve	43
幅	fù	a measure word	44
阜城門	Fùchéngmén	name of a place in Beijing	47

g

改	gǎi	to correct	47
蓋兒	gàir	cover; lid	42
肝	gān	liver	32
乾凈	gānjìng	clean; neat and tidy	48
感動	gǎndòng	to move; to touch; moving	49
感冒	gǎnmào	to catch cold; （common） cold	46
感想	gǎnxiǎng	impressions; feeling	47
幹	gàn	to work; to do	42
剛	gāng	just; only a short while ago	38
鋼鐵學院	Gāngtiě Xuéyuàn	The Beijing Iron & Steel Engineering Institute	38
高	gāo	tall	37
各	gè	each; every; various; respectively	43
個子	gèzi	height; stature; build	32
工地	gōngdì	construction site	42
公分	gōngfēn	a measure word, centimeter	37
公共	gōnggòng	public	38

公共汽車	gōnggòngqìchē	bus	38
恭賀新禧	gōnghèxīnxǐ	Happy New Year	48
公斤	gōngjīn	kilogram （kg. ）	42
公園	gōngyuán	park	33
够	gòu	enough; sufficient	43
古	gǔ	ancient	33
鼓掌	gǔzhǎng	to applaud	40
故宮	gùgōng	the Imperial Palace	41
故居	gùjū	former residence	47
顧客	gùkè	customer	43
故事	gùshi	story	38
顧問	gùwèn	adviser	42
刮（風）	guā（fēng）	to blow （said of wind）	35
掛	guà	to hang; to put up	34
掛號	guàhào	to register （a letter, etc. ）	34
掛號證	guàhàozhèng	register card	46
拐彎	guǎiwuān	to turn a corner	38
關	guān	to close; to shut	46
關心	guānxīn	to care for; to be concerned with	39
觀衆	guānzhòng	spectator; audience	40
廣播	guǎngbō	to broadcast	40
廣播室	guǎngbōshì	broadcasting room	41
廣播員	guǎngbōyuán	radio（or wire-broadcasting）announcer	41
廣場	guǎngchǎng	spuare	41
廣州	Guǎngzhōu	name of a city	44
貴	guì	expensive	36
櫃台	guìtái	counter	34
國際	guójì	international	31
過	guò	to come over; to pass by	41
過	guò	a structural particle	32

h

海	hǎi	sea	50
寒假	hánjià	winter vacation	35
喊	hǎn	to shout	44
航空	hángkōng	air （mail）	34
好吃	hǎochī	delicious; tasty	43
合唱	héchàng	chorus; to chorus	49
合適	héshì	suitable, fit	37
黑暗	hēi'àn	dark	49

紅蓮	hónglián	red lotus	50
紅綠燈	hónglǜdēng	(red & green) traffic light	38
紅葉	hóngyè	red autumnal leaves (of maple, etc.)	33
厚	hòu	thick	36
後來	hòulái	afterwards; later	45
壺	hú	pot, a measure word	36
湖	hú	lake	44
胡同	hútòng	lane; alley	38
護士	hùshì	nurse	46
護照	hùzhào	passport	31
花	huā	to spend (money)	37
華表	huábiǎo	marble pillar (an ornamental column erected in front of palaces, tombs, etc.)	42
華僑	huáqiáo	overseas Chinese	31
話	huà	words; talk	31
畫	huà	to paint, to draw	36
畫兒	huàr	picture; painting	36
話劇	huàjù	spoken drama	49
畫蛇添足	huàshétiānzú	(fig.) ruin the effect by adding what is superfluous	36
畫展	huàzhǎn	art exhibition	50
懷念	huáiniàn	to cherish the memory of; to think of	47
壞	huài	bad; there is somthing wrong with	49
歡迎	huānyíng	to welcome	49
換	huàn	to change	38
黃	huáng	a surname	48
皇帝	huángdì	emperor	41
灰	huī	grey	37
恢復	huīfù	to recover	47
活	huó	to live; alive; living	47
活兒	huór	work; job	42
貨	huò	goods; commodity	36

j

迹	jī	trace; track; sign	33
激動	jīdòng	excited	40
機會	jīhuì	chance; opportunity	35
…極了	jíle	extremely; exceedingly	40
擠	jǐ	crowded; to squeeze	41
寄	jì	to post; to mail	34

記	jì	to remember; to bear in mind	39
記録	jìlù	record	40
紀念	jìniàn	to commemorate; commemoration	47
假期	jiàqī	vacation	35
價錢	jiàqián	price	36
間	jiān	a measure word	47
檢查	jiǎnchá	check up; physical examination	32
簡樸	jiǎnpǔ	simple and unadorned	47
建設	jiànshè	to build; to construct; construction	31
建築	jiànzhù	building; to build; to construct	41
江西	Jiāngxī	name of a Chinese province	36
講	jiǎng	tell; speak; explain （text, etc.）	38
講解	jiǎngjiě	to explain	47
講解員	jiǎngjiěyuán	guide	47
獎狀	jiǎngzhuàng	certificate of merit	42
交	jiāo	to pay （money）	37
脚	jiáo	foot	41
餃子	jiǎozi	dumpling	46
叫	jiào	a preposition	49
街	jiē	street	38
接	jiē	to extend; to connect	47
街道	jiēdào	street	39
節	jié	festival	48
節目	jiémù	programme; item	49
節日	jiérì	festival; holiday	48
解	jiě	to relieve oneself	46
解放	jiěfàng	to liberate	36
借	jiè	to borrow; to lend	49
近	jìn	near	44
景德鎮	Jǐngdézhèn	name of a Chinese city	36
景山	Jǐngshān	name of a hill in Jingshan park	41
景山公園	Jǐngshān Gōngyuán	name of a park in Beijng	41
鏡頭	jìngtóu	camera lens	42
鏡子	jìngzi	mirror	44
句	jù	a measure word, for sentences or lines of verse	39
劇場	jùchǎng	theatre	49
絶	jué	disappear, vanish; by no means	33
覺得	juéde	to think; to feel	33
决定	juédìng	to decide; decision	44

k

開會	kāihuì	to hold or attend a meeting	31
開學	kāixué	school opens; new term begins	35
開演	kāiyǎn	(of a play, movie, etc.) to begin	49
看（病）	kàn (bìng)	to see (a doctor, etc.)	35
考	kǎo	to test	35
考試	kǎoshì	to test; examination	35
科	kē	department (of internal medicine, etc.)	46
咳嗽	késou	to cough	46
渴	kě	thirsty	43
可愛	kě'ài	lovely	45
可能	kěnéng	may; probable; possible	46
可笑	kěxiào	funny; rediculous	45
客人	kèren	guest; visitor	39
塊（元）	kuài (yuán)	a measure word (a Chinese monetary unit, equal to 10 jiao or mao)	36
寬	kuān	wide	42
昆明湖	Kūnmíng Hú	Kunming Lake	44

l

拉	lā	to play (string instruments)	31
藍	lán	blue	37
蘭花	lánhuā	cymbidium; orchid	50
勞動	láodòng	to labor; to work	49
老	lǎo	old; aged	31
老虎	lǎohǔ	tiger	47
老驥伏櫪，志在千里	lǎojìfúlì zhìzàiqiānlí	an old steed in the stable still aspires to gallop a thousand li; (fig.) old people may still cherish high aspirations	39
姥姥	lǎolao	maternal grandmother, grandma	46
老舍	lǎoshě	name of a person	49
累	lèi	to feel tired	43
冷	lěng	cold	33
禮堂	lǐtáng	assembly hall; auditorium	42
禮物	lǐwù	gift; present	48
李自成	Lǐ Zìchéng	name of a person	41
立	lì	to stand; to erect	33
厲害	lìhai	serious; terrible	46
立刻	lìkè	immediately; at once	46

麗麗	lìlì	name of a person	45
歷史	lìshǐ	history	36
利用	lìyòng	to use; to make use of	35
連…也…	lián…yě…	even	49
量	liáng	to measure	32
涼快	liángkuài	nice and cold; pleasantly cool	33
糧食	liángshí	grain; food	48
輛	liàng	a measure word for vehicles	37
亮	liàng	light; bright	43
了	liǎo	to end up	42
料子	liàozi	material	37
鄰居	línjū	neighbor	39
臨摹	línmó	to copy (a model of calligraphy or painting, etc.)	50
零	líng	zero	36
零錢	língqián	change (said of money)	36
留	liú	remain; ask somebody to stay	39
留言	liúyán	leave one's comments or a message	47
留言簿	liúyánbù	visitors' book	47
隆冬	lóngdōng	midwinter; the depth of winter	33
路	lù	road; way	31
路口	lùkǒu	crossing; intersection	38
録音	lùyīn	to record; recording	46
旅館	lǚguǎn	hotel	41
旅行	lǚxíng	to travel	44
緑燈	lǜdēng	green light	43
駱駝祥子	Luòtuó Xiángzi	name of a novel	49

m

麻煩	máfan	to bother; troublesome	48
馬	mǎ	horse	38
馬路	mǎlù	road; street	38
賣	mài	to sell	49
毛衣	máoyī	woollen sweater	37
毛主席	Máo Zhǔxí	Chairman Mao	42
貿易	màoyì	trade	44
没關系	méiguānxi	it doesn't matter	41
梅花	méihuā	plum blossom	33
美	měi	beautiful	41
美國	Měiguó	the United States (of America)	31

門口	ménkǒu	doorway; entrance	41
米	mǐ	a measure word, meter	37
棉襖	mián'ǎo	cotton-padded jacket	37
面兒	miànr	cover; outside	37
秒	miǎo	a measure word, second	40
民樂	mínyuè	music; esp. folk music, for traditional instruments	49
名	míng	a measure word	40
明信片	míngxìnpiàn	postcard	34
摩托車	mótuōchē	motorcycle	41
墨鏡	mòjìng	sunglasses	45
母親	mǔqin	mother	44

n

拿	ná	to get; to take	32
南邊	nánbiān	south; southern part	38
南京	Nánjīng	Nanjing （city）	34
南亞	Nán Yà	South Asia	45
南轅北轍	nányuánběizhé	（fig.） act in a way that defeats one's purpose	38
男子	nánzǐ	man	40
內科	nèikē	medical department	32
年	nián	New Year	48
年畫兒	niánhuàr	New Year （or Spring Festival） picture	48
年夜飯	niányèfàn	New Year's Eve family dinner	48
牛	niú	ox; cattle	47
牛奶	niúnǎi	milk	43
女高音	nǚgāoyīn	soprano	49
暖和	nuǎnhuo	warm; nice and warm	33

p

爬	pá	to climb	44
怕	pà	to be afraid; to fear	33
排隊	páiduì	to line up	38
牌子	páizi	sign; plate	34
彷徨	Pánghuáng	name of a collection of short stories	47
胖	pàng	fat; stout; plump	37
跑	pǎo	to run	38
培養	péiyǎng	to foster; to bring up	47
篇	piān	a measure word	47

便宜	piányi	cheap	36
片	piàn	a measure word, tablets	46
平安里	Píng'ānlǐ	name of a street in Beijing	38
平方米	píngfāngmǐ	square meter	42
平信	píngxìn	ordinary mail	34

q

騎	qí	to ride （a bicycle）	37
齊白石	Qí Bǎishí	name of a person	36
奇怪	qíguài	surprised; strange	35
旗袍	qípāo	Chinese-style frock	37
旗子	qízi	flag; banner	40
汽車	qìchē	automobile; car	38
千	qiān	thousand	42
錢	qián	money	35
牆	qiáng	wall	34
敲	qiāo	to knock （at a door）	33
橋	qiáo	bridge	44
親愛	qīn'ài	dear	48
親切	qīnqiè	cordial; kind	43
青	qīng	green	44
清楚	qīngchu	clear	41
青年	qīngnián	youth	47
晴	qíng	（of weather） fine; bright; clear	33
情況	qíngkuàng	condition; situation; state of affairs	35
屈服	qūfú	to surrender; to yield	33
全	quán	whole	48
群衆	qūnzhòng	mass; people	47

r

讓	ràng	a preposition	49
熱	rè	hot	33
熱烈	rèliè	warm; enthusiastic	40
人民大會堂	Rénmín Dàhuìtáng	Great Hall of the People	42
人民英雄紀念碑	Rénmín Yīngxióng Jìniànbēi	Monument to the People's Heroes	42
人物	rénwù	figure; characters（in a play, etc.）	44
日記	rìjì	diary	49

s/sh

三國演義	Sānguóyǎnyì	name of a novel, "Romance of the Three Kingdoms"	44
三里河	Sānlǐhé	name of a street in Beijing	38
三里屯	Sānlǐtún	name of a street in Beijing	38
掃	sǎo	to sweep	48
殺	shā	to kill	49
山	shān	hill; mountain	41
上（次）	shàng（cì）	last（time）; a previous（occasion）	37
上海	Shànghǎi	Shanghai	31
社會	shèhuì	society	49
社會主義	shèhuìzhǔyì	socialism	31
設計	shèjì	to design	47
生	shēng	to be born	44
生產	shēngchǎn	to produce; to manufacture	36
生活	shēnghuó	life; to live	47
生命	shēngmìng	life	32
聖誕節	shèngdànjié	Christmas Day	48
詩	shī	poem; poetry; verse	33
師傅	shīfu	master worker	43
獅子	shīzi	lion	42
石（頭）	shí（tou）	stone; rock	42
時間	shíjiān	（duration of）time;（a point of）time	31
實現	shíxiàn	to realize; to achieve	31
使者	shǐzhě	emissary; envoy	45
市	shì	city	34
世界	shìjiè	the world	50
逝世	shìshì	to pass away	50
收	shōu	to receive	34
收據	shōujù	receipt	34
收拾	shōushi	to put in order; to tidy up	48
收音機	shōuyīnjī	radio	34
首	shǒu	a measure word	33
手	shǒu	hand	46
首都	shǒudū	capital of a country	31
首都國際機場	Shǒudū Guójì Jīchǎng	the Capital International Airprot, Beijing	31
首都劇場	Shǒudū Jùchǎng	the Capital Theatre	49
手續	shǒuxù	formalities	31

瘦	shòu	tight; thin; lean	37
售貨員	shòuhuòyuán	shop assistant	36
售票處	shòupiàochù	ticket office; booking office	41
售票員	shòupiàoyuán	ticket seller; conductor	38
舒服	shūfu	comfortable; well	46
書架	shūjià	bookshelf	39
叔叔	shūshu	father's younger brother; uncle	39
暑假	shǔjià	summer vacation	35
樹	shù	tree	33
説明書	shuōmíngshū	synopsis （of a play or film）	49
司機	sījī	driver	41
死	sǐ	to die	41
雖然	suīrán	though; although	39
歲數	suìshu	age	42
所以	suǒyǐ	so; therefore; as a result	44

t

它	tā	it	44
它們	tāmen	they （refers to things, animals）	45
塔	tǎ	pagoda	44
太極拳	tàijíquán	a kind of traditional Chinese shadowboxing	40
太陽	tàiyáng	the sun	44
探親	tànqīn	to go home to visit one's family	44
糖	táng	sugar	43
唐山	Tángshān	name of a city	36
躺	tǎng	to lie	36
套	tào	a measure word, set	36
疼	téng	ache; pain; sore	46
藤野	Téngyě	name of a person	47
提	tí	to suggest; to put forward	43
提高	tígāo	to increase; to improve	36
體温	tǐwēn	（body） temperature	46
天	tiān	sky; heaven	44
天安門	Tiān'ānmén	Tian'anmen（Gate of Heavenly Peace）	34
天安門廣場	Tiān'ánmén Guǎngchǎng	Tiananmen Square	41
天氣	tiānqì	weather	31
填	tián	to fill	32
條子	tiáozi	a short note; a slip of paper	39

跳	tiào	to jump	44
貼	tiē	to paste	48
聽説	tīngshuō	it is said that	41
挺立	tǐnglì	to stand erect; to stand upright	50
亭子	tíngzi	pavilion	41
同志	tóngzhì	comrade	31
頭	tóu	head	45
頭發	tóufa	hair （on human head）	32
透視	tòushì	to examine by fluoroscope; to take X-ray examination	32
圖片	túpiàn	picture; photograph	34
兔子	tùzi	hare; rabbit	48
團聚	tuánjù	to reunite; to have a reunion	48
推	tuī	to push	43
腿	tuǐ	leg	45
退休	tuìxiū	to retire	39

W

襪子	wàzi	socks; stockings	37
外國	wàiguó	foreign country	45
豌豆趙	Wǎndòu Zhào	name of a person	43
豌豆粥	wǎndòu zhōu	pea gruel	43
完	wán	to finish; to be over	39
完成	wánchéng	to complete; to finish	42
碗	wǎn	bowl; a measure word, bowl	36
萬	wàn	ten thousand	42
萬壽山	Wànshòu Shān	Longevity Hill	44
往	wǎng	to go （to a place）	38
往	wàng	toward; （train） bound for	33
微笑	wēixiào	to smile	50
尾巴	wěiba	tail	47
偉大	wěidà	great	47
胃	wèi	stomach	32
爲甚麽	wèi shénme	why	34
文學家	wénxuéjiā	writer; man of letters	47
文章	wénzhāng	writings	47
屋子	wūzi	room	48
舞蹈	wǔdǎo	dance	49
霧	wù	fog; mist	33

X

西邊	xībiān	west; western part	41
西三條	Xīsāntiáo	name of a place in Beijing	47
希望	xīwàng	to hope; to wish; hope; wish	31
吸引	xīyǐn	to attrack; to draw	49
西裝	xīzhuāng	Western-style suit	37
習慣	xíguàn	to be used to; to be accustomed to; habit; custom	33
洗	xǐ	to wash	41
洗（照片）	xǐ（zhàopiàn）	to develope （a film）	42
下	xià	to get off （bus, etc）	38
下（星期）	xià（xīngqī）	next （week）	37
下（雨）	xià（yǔ）	to rain	33
下邊	xiàbiān	below; under; underneath	34
夏歷	xiàlì	the traditional Chinese calendar	48
先	xiān	first	32
現代化	xiàndàihuà	modernization	31
香山	Xiāng Shān	Fragrance Hill （Park）	33
象	xiàng	elephant	45
嚮導	xiàngdǎo	guide	41
小吃	xiǎochī	snack; refreshments	43
小吃店	xiǎochīdiàn	snack bar; lunch room	43
小冬	Xiǎodōng	name of a child	42
小紅	Xiǎohóng	name of a child	42
小蘭	Xiǎolán	name of a person	39
小聲	xiǎoshēng	in a low voice;（speak）in whispers	46
小時	xiǎoshí	hour	31
小說	xiǎoshuō	novel; short story	41
小提琴	xiǎotíqín	violin	31
辛苦	xīnkǔ	hard; exhausting; with much toil	31
新年	xīnnián	new year	48
心臟	xīnzàng	heart	32
信封	xìnfēng	envelope	34
信箱	xìnxiāng	post-office box （P.O.B.）; letter box; mail box	34
姓名	xìngmíng	full name; surname and given name	34
杏仁	xìngrén	almond	43
杏仁豆腐	xìngréndòufu	almond junket	43
熊猫	xióngmāo	panda	45
熊猫館	xióngmāoguǎn	panda exhibition hall	45

修	xiū	to build （road, etc）; to repair	38
修建	xiūjiàn	to build; to construct	42
選舉	xuǎnjǔ	to elect	39
學期	xuéqī	term; semester	35
學校	xuéxiào	school	31
雪	xuě	snow	33
血	xuè	blood	32
血壓	xuèyā	blood pressure	32

y

亞洲	Yà Zhōu	Asia	45
顏色	yánsè	color	37
演	yǎn	to perform; to play; to act	49
演出	yǎnchū	to perform; to put on a show; performance; show	49
眼睛	yǎnjīng	eye	32
演員	yǎnyuán	actor or actress; performer	49
陽陽	Yángyáng	name of a child	48
樣子	yàngzi	manner; air; looks	45
藥	yào	medicine	46
要不	yàobù	or; or else; otherwise	37
藥方	yàofāng	prescription	46
藥劑士	yàojìshī	druggist; pharmacist	46
要是	yàoshì	if	41
爺爺	yéye	grandpa	42
野草	yěcǎo	name of a collection of prose poems	47
頁	yè	page; a measure word, page	50
葉子	yèzi	leaf	33
衣服	yīfu	clothes; clothing	37
衣櫃	yīguì	wardrobe	39
一...就...	yī...jiù...	no sooner than; as soon as	39
醫務所	yīwùsuǒ	clinic	32
醫院	yīyuàn	hospital	46
遺產	yíchǎn	heritage	47
一共	yígòng	altogether; in all	36
頤和園	Yíhéyuán	Summer Palace	33
一會兒	yíhuìr	a little while	41
一樣	yíyàng	same; identical	37
已經	yǐjīng	already	31
以前	yǐqián	before; in the past	32

意見	yìjiàn	criticism; comment or suggestions	43
藝術	yìshù	art	42
藝術家	yìshùjiā	artist	49
意思	yìsi	meaning	39
陰天	yīntiān	cloudy day; overcast sky	33
因爲	yīnwèi	because; for	48
迎春花	yíngchūnhuā	winter jasmine	50
營業	yíngyè	to do business	34
營業員	yíngyèyuán	clerk; shop assistant	34
永遠	yóngyuǎn	always; forever	39
油餅	yóubǐng	deep-fried pancake	43
郵局	yóujú	post office	34
郵票	yóupiào	stamp	34
有的	yǒude	some	34
有（一）點兒	yǒu（yì）diǎnr	a bit	43
愉快	yúkuài	happy; delighted	39
雨	yǔ	rain	33
語言	yǔyán	language	31
雨衣	yǔyī	raincoat	37
玉	yù	jade	36
預報	yùbào	forecast	33
園林	yuánlín	gardens; park; landscape garden	44
元宵	yuánxiāo	sweet dumplings made of glutinous rice flour	43
元宵節	Yuánxiāo Jié	the Lantern Festival	48
遠方	yuǎnfāng	distant place	39
院子	yuànzi	courtyard	47
運動	yùndòng	to exercise （oneself）; sport	40
運動會	yùndònghuì	sports meet	40
運動員	yùndòngyuán	sportsman; player	40

z/zh

咱們	zǎnmen	we	38
棗樹	zǎoshù	jujube tree; date tree	47
怎麼	zěnme	how; why	38
炸糕	zhágāo	fried cake	43
站	zhàn	stop	38
張華光	Zhāng Huáguāng	name of a person	31
張華明	Zhāng Huámíng	name of a person	41

掌櫃	zhǎngguì	shopkeeper	49
著急	zháo jí	feel anxiously	35
找（錢）	zhǎo（qián）	to give change	36
照相機	zhàoxiàngjī	camera	41
這麼	zhème	so; such	42
這樣	zhèyàng	so; such; like this	32
著	zhe	a particle	34
針	zhēn	injection; needle	46
珍貴	zhēnguì	precious; valuable	45
整齊	zhěngqí	neat; tidy	48
挣	zhèng	to earn; to make （money）	35
正常	zhèngcháng	normal; regular	32
正確	zhèngquè	correct; right	49
之	zhī	a modal particle; a pronoun	43
只	zhī	a measure word	45
枝	zhī	a measure word	50
知識	zhīshì	knowledge	32
...之一	...zhīyī	one of ...	49
指	zhǐ	to point at; to point to	34
只	zhǐ	only	36
只有	zhǐyǒu	only	44
質量	zhìliàng	quality	36
鐘	zhōng	clock	31
終點	zhōngdiǎn	terminal point; terminus	38
中國歷史博物館	Zhōngguó Lìshǐ Bówùguǎn	Museum of Chinese History	42
中國美術館	Zhōngguó Měishù Guǎn	National Art Gallery	50
中間	zhōngjiān	center; middle	42
中山裝	zhōngshān-zhuāng	Chinese tunic suit	37
中式	zhōngshì	Chinese style	37
種	zhǒng	a measure word, kind; type	36
重	zhòng	heavy	42
種	zhòng	to grow; to plant	46
粥	zhōu	gruel; porridge	43
周到	zhōudào	thoughtful; considerate	41
周恩來	Zhōu Ēnlái	Zhou Enlai	50
周年	zhōunián	anniversary	50
周總理	Zhōu Zǒnglǐ	Premier Zhou	50
株	zhū	a measure word	47

竹（子）	zhú（zi）	bamboo	45
主任	zhǔrèn	director; head	39
主席	zhǔxí	chairman	40
主席台	zhǔxítái	rostrum; platform	40
住院	zhùyuàn	to be in hospital; to be hospitalized	46
抓	zhuā	to arrest; to catch; to clutch	49
專業	zhuānyè	specialty; specialized suject	35
自行車	zìxíngchē	bicycle; bike	36
總理	zónglǐ	premier	50
嘴	zuī	mouth	32
最	zuì	best; most; least; to the highest（lowest）degree	33
最後	zuìhòu	last	50
最近	zuìjìn	recently; lately	32
作	zuò	to regard as; to take（somebody）for	47
座	zuò	a measure word	44
作品	zuòpǐn	works （of literature and art）	49
座位	zuòwèi	seat	38

APPENDIX II

English	Pinyin	Character	Lesson
a			
a bit	yǒu (yì) diǎr	有(一)點兒	43
a little while	yíhuìr	一會兒	41
abundant	fēngfù	豐富	47
ache	téng	疼	46
achieve	shíxiàn	實現	31
achievement	chéngjī	成績	35
act (e.g. in movies)	yǎn	演	37
act in a way that defeats one's purpose (fig.)	nányuánběizhé	南轅北轍	38
actor/actress	yǎnyuán	演員	49
adviser	gùwèn	顧問	42
Africa	Fēizhōu	非洲	45
afterwards	hòulái	後來	45
age	suìshu	歲數	42
aged	lǎo	老	31
air (one's bearings)	yàngzi	樣子	45
air (mail)	hángkōng	航空	34
alley	hútòng	胡同	38
almond	xìngrén	杏仁	43
almond junket	xìngréndòufu	杏仁豆腐	43
already	yǐjīng	已經	31
although	suīrán	雖然	39
altogether	yígòng	一共	36
always	yǒngyuǎn	永遠	39
ancient	gǔ	古	33
animal	dòngwù	動物	45
anniversary	zhōunián	周年	50
another	biéde	別的	43
applaud	gúzhǎng	鼓掌	40
arrest	zhuā	抓	49
art	yìshù	藝術	42
art exhibition	huàzhǎn	畫展	50
artist	yìshùjiā	藝術家	49
as a result	suǒyǐ	所以	44
as soon as	yī...jiù...	一...就...	39

Asia	Yà Zhōu	亚洲	45
ask somebody to stay	liú	留	39
assembly hall	lǐtáng	禮堂	42
at once	lìkè	立刻	46
athlete	yùndòngyuán	運動員	40
attend a meeting	kāihuì	開會	31
attrack	xīyǐn	吸引	49
audience	guānzhòng	觀衆	40
auditorium	lǐtáng	禮堂	42
aunt	dàniáng	大娘	38
auntie	āyí	阿姨	39
automobile	qìchē	汽車	38

b

bad	huài	壞	49
bag	dài	袋	48
bamboo	zhú (zi)	竹 (子)	45
banner	qízi	旗子	40
be accustomed to	xíguàn	習慣	37
be afraid	pà	怕	33
be away on official business	chūchāi	出差	44
be born	shēng	生	44
be concerned with	guānxīn	關心	39
be hospitalized, in hospital	zhùyuàn	住院	46
be on a business trip	chūchāi	出差	44
be over	wán	完	39
be used to	xíguàn	習慣	37
bean curd	dòufu	豆腐	43
bear in mind	jì	記	39
beautiful	měi	美	41
because	yīnwèi	因爲	48
become	chéng	成	47
before	yǐqián	以前	32
begin (of play/movie)	kāiyǎn	開演	49
Beihai Park	Běihǎi	北海	32
Beijing Iron & Steel Engineering Institute	Gāngtiě Xuéyuàn	鋼鐵學院	38
Beijing Languages Institute	Běijīng Yǔyán Xuéyuàn	北京語言學院	31

Beijing Zoo	Běijīng Dòngwùyuán	北京動物園	45
below	xiàbiān	下邊	34
besides	chúle...yǐwài	除了...以外	47
best	zuì	最	33
bill	dān	單	34
blood	xuè	血	32
blood preasure	xuèyā	血壓	32
blow (said of wind)	guā (fēng)	刮（風）	35
blue	lán	藍	37
boat	chuán	船	44
body temperature	tǐwēn	體温	46
book	běnzi	本子	39
booking office	shòupiàochù	售票處	41
bookshelf	shūjià	書架	39
borrow	jiè	借	49
bother	máfan	麻煩	48
bound for (said of train)	wàng	往	38
bowl	wǎn	碗	36
bowl (as measure word)	wǎn	碗	36
boy or girl friend	duìxiàng	對象	44
break	dǎpò	打破	40
bridge	qiáo	橋	44
bright	cōngming	聰明	39
bright	liàng	亮	43
bright (weather)	qíng	晴	33
bring up	péiyǎng	培養	47
bring (with)	dài	帶	38
broadcast	guǎngbō	廣播	40
broadcasting room	guǎngbōshì	廣播室	41
build	jiànshè	建設	31
build	jiànzhù	建築	41
build (road, etc.)	xiū	修	38
build	xiūjiàn	修建	42
building	jiànzhù	建築	41
bus	gōnggòngqìchē	公共汽車	38
but	dànshì	但是	39
by no means	jué	絶	33
bicycle/bike	zìxíngchē	自行車	36

C

cab	chūzūqìchē	出租汽車	38
cable	diànbào	電報	34
camera	zhàoxiàngjī	照相機	41
camera lens	jìngtóu	鏡頭	42
Capital International Airport, Beijing	Shǒudū Guójì Jīchǎng	首都國際機場	31
Capital Theatre	Shǒudū Jùchǎng	首都劇場	49
capital of a country	shǒudū	首都	31
car	qìchē	汽車	38
care for	guānxīn	關心	39
catch	zhuā	抓	49
catch cold	gǎnmào	感冒	46
cattle	niú	牛	47
center	zhōngjiān	中間	42
centimeter	gōngfēn	公分	37
certificate of merit	jiǎngzhuàng	獎狀	42
chairman	zhǔxí	主席	40
Chairman Mao	Máo Zhǔxí	毛主席	42
chance	jīhuì	機會	35
change	huàn	換	38
change （said of money）	língqián	零錢	36
characters（in plays/novels）	rénwù	人物	44
cheap	piányi	便宜	36
check up	jiǎnchá	檢查	32
Chen Yi	Chén Yì	陳毅	33
cherish the memory of	huáiniàn	懷念	47
chinaware	cíqì	瓷器	36
Chinese style	zhōngshì	中式	37
Chinese-style frock	qípáo	旗袍	37
Chinese tunic suit	zhōngshānzhuāng	中山裝	37
chorus	héchàng	合唱	49
Christmas Day	shèngdànjié	聖誕節	48
city	shì	市	34
class	bān	班	42
clean	gānjing	乾净	48
clean up	dǎsǎo	打掃	48
clear	qīngchu	清楚	41
clear（weather）	qíng	晴	33
clerk	yíngyèyuán	營業員	34
climb	pá	爬	44
clinic	yīwùsuǒ	醫務所	32

clock	zhōng	鐘	31
close	guān	關	46
cloth shoes	bùxié	布鞋	37
clothes	yīfu	衣服	37
clothing	yīfu	衣服	37
cloudy day	yīntiān	陰天	33
clutch	zhuā	抓	49
cold	lěng	冷	33
college	dàxué	大學	31
color	yánsè	顏色	45
colored flag	cǎiqí	彩旗	40
come out	chū	出	31
come over	guò	過	41
comfortable	shūfu	舒服	46
commemorate	jìniàn	紀念	47
commemoration	jìniàn	紀念	47
comment or suggestions	yìjiàn	意見	43
commodity	huò	貨	36
common cold	gǎnmào	感冒	46
comparatively	bǐjiào	比較	43
compare	bǐjiào	比較	43
compel	bī	逼	32
complete	wánchéng	完成	42
comrade	tóngzhì	同志	31
condition	qíngkuàng	情況	35
conductor (on bus)	shoupiaoyuan	售票員	41
connect	jiē	接	47
considerate	zhōudào	周到	41
construct	xiūjiàn	修建	42
construct	jiànshè	建設	31
construct	jiànzhù	建築	41
construction	jiànshè	建設	31
construction site	gōngdì	工地	42
contract a disease	dé (bìng)	得（病）	32
convenient	fāngbiàn	方便	42
copy (a model of calligraphy/painting)	línmó	臨摹	50
cordial	qīnqiè	親切	43
correct	zhèngquè	正確	49
correct something	gǎi	改	47
cotton cloth	bù	布	34

cotton-padded jacket	miáo'ǎo	棉襖	37
cough	kēsou	咳嗽	46
counter	guìtái	櫃台	34
courtyard	yuànzi	院子	47
cover	miànr	面兒	37
cover	gàir	蓋兒	42
criticism	yìjiàn	意見	43
cross (a street)	chuān (mǎlù)	穿（馬路）	43
crossing	lùkǒu	路口	38
crowded	jǐ	擠	41
custom	fēngsú	風俗	48
custom	xíguàn	習慣	37
customer	gùkè	顧客	43
cymbidium	lánhuā	蘭花	50

d

dance	wǔdǎo	舞蹈	49
dark	hēi'àn	黑暗	49
date tree	zǎoshù	棗樹	47
dear	qīn'ài	親愛	48
decide	juédìng	決定	44
decision	juédìng	決定	44
deep-fried pancake	yóubǐng	油餅	43
degree	dù	度	33
delicious	hǎochī	好吃	43
delighted	yúkuài	愉快	39
department (of internal medicine, etc.)	kē	科	46
Department Store	bǎihuòdàlóu	百貨大樓	36
depth of winter	lóngdōng	隆冬	33
design	shèjì	設計	47
develop	fāzhǎn	發展	36
develop (a film)	xǐ (zhàopiàn)	洗（照片）	42
diary	rìjì	日記	49
die	sǐ	死	41
direction	fāngxiàng	方向	38
director	zhǔrèn	主任	39
disappear	jué	絶	33
distant place	yuǎnfāng	遠方	39
do	gàn	幹	42

do business	yíngyè	營業	34
doorway	ménkǒu	門口	41
draw	huà	畫	36
driver	sījī	司機	41
druggist	yàojìshī	藥劑士	46
dumpling	jiǎozi	餃子	46
duration of time	shíjiān	時間	31

e

each	gè	各	43
ear	ěrduo	耳朵	43
earn	zhèng	掙	35
east	dōngbiān	東邊	38
eastern part	dōngbiān	東邊	38
edge (of a lake, etc.)	biān	邊	44
elect	xuǎnjǔ	選舉	39
elephant	xiàng	象	45
emmissary	shǐzhě	使者	45
emperor	huángdì	皇帝	41
Emperor Chongzhen	Chóngzhēn	崇禎	41
end up	liǎo	了	42
enough	gòu	够	43
enrich	fēngfù	豐富	47
enthusiastic	rèliè	熱烈	40
entrance	ménkǒu	門口	41
envelope	xìnfēng	信封	34
envoy	shǐzhě	使者	45
errect	lì	立	33
even	lián...yě...	連...也...	49
every	gè	各	43
examine by fluoroscope	tòushì	透視	32
examination	kǎoshì	考試	35
exceedingly	jíle	...極了	40
except	chúle...yǐwài	除了...以外	47
excited	jīdòng	激動	40
exercise (oneself)	yùndòng	運動	40
exhausting	xīnkǔ	辛苦	31
expensive	guì	貴	44
explain	jiǎngjiě	講解	47
explain (text, etc.)	jiǎng	講	38

extend	jiē	接	47
extremely	jíle	…極了	40
eye	yǎnjing	眼睛	49

f

fall ill	dé (bìng)	得 (病)	32
fat	pàng	胖	37
fat	féi	肥	37
fear	pà	怕	33
feel	juéde	覺得	33
feel anxiously	zháojí	著急	35
feel embarrassed	bù hǎoyìsi	不好意思	39
feel embarrassing (to do something)	bù hǎoyìsi	不好意思	39
feel tired	lèi	累	43
feeling	gǎnxiǎng	感想	47
festival	jié	節	48
festival	jiérì	節日	48
figures (in plays/novels)	rénwù	人物	44
fill	tián	填	32
fine (weather)	qíng	晴	33
finish	wán	完	39
finish	wánchéng	完成	42
fircracker	bàozhú	爆竹	48
first	xiān	先	32
fit	héshì	合適	37
flag	qízi	旗子	40
fog	wù	霧	33
folk music (for traditional instruments)	mínyuè	民樂	49
food	liángshí	糧食	48
foot	jiǎo	脚	41
for	yīnwèi	因爲	48
for	duì	對	39
force	bī	逼	32
forecast	yùbào	預報	33
foreign country	wàiguó	外國	45
forever	yǒngyuǎn	永遠	39
form	biǎo	表	32
form	dān	單	34
formalities	shǒuxù	手續	31

former residence	gùjū	故居	47
foster	péiyǎng	培養	47
Fragrance Hill （park）	Xiāng Shān	香山	33
fried cake	zhágāo	炸糕	43
full name	xìngmíng	姓名	34
funny	kěxiào	可笑	45

g

gardens	yuánlín	園林	44
get	ná	拿	32
get off （bus, etc.）	xià	下	38
gift	lǐwù	禮物	48
give an injection	dǎ（zhēn）	打（針）	46
give change	zhǎo（qián）	找（錢）	36
go home to visit one's family	tànqīn	探親	44
go out	chū	出	31
go （to a place）	wàng	往	38
goods	huò	貨	36
graduate	bìyè	畢業	44
grain	liángshí	糧食	48
grandpa	yéye	爺爺	42
grass	cǎo	草	44
great	wěidà	偉大	32
Great Hall of the People	Rénmín Dàhuìtáng	人民大會堂	42
Great Wall	Chángchēng	長城	32
green	qīng	青	44
green light	lǜdēng	綠燈	43
grey	huī	灰	37
grow	zhòng	種	46
gruel	zhōu	粥	43
guest	kèren	客人	39
guide	jiǎngjiěyuán	講解員	47
guide	xiàngdǎo	嚮導	41

h

habit	xíguàn	習慣	33
hair （on human head）	tóufa	頭髮	32
hand	shǒu	手	46
hang	diào	吊	41

hang	guà	掛	34
happy	yúkuài	愉快	39
Happy New Year	gōnghèxīnxǐ	恭賀新禧	48
hard	xīnkǔ	辛苦	31
hare	tùzi	兔子	48
have a check-up	jiǎnchá	檢查	32
have a fever	fāshāo	發燒	46
have a holiday/vocation	fàng (jià)	放 (假)	35
have a reunion	tuánjù	團聚	48
have an injection	dǎ (zhēn)	打 (針)	46
have something made	dìngzuò	定作	37
head	tóu	頭	45
head (of a department)	zhǔrèn	主任	39
heart	xīn	心	32
heaven	tián	天	44
heavy	zhòng	重	42
height/build	gèzi	個子	32
heritage	yíchǎn	遺産	47
hill	shān	山	41
history	lìshǐ	歷史	36
hold a meeting	kāihuì	開會	31
holiday	jiérì	節日	48
hope (as noun & verb)	xīwàng	希望	31
horse	mǎ	馬	38
hospital	yīyuàn	醫院	46
hot	rè	熱	33
hotel	lǚguǎn	旅館	41
hour	xiǎoshí	小時	31
how	duōme	多麼	44
how	zěnme	怎麼	38
human excrement	dàbiàn	大便	46
hundred	bǎi	百	33
hungry	è	餓	43

i

ice-lolly	bīnggùnr	冰棍兒	42
ice-sucker	bīnggùnr	冰棍兒	42
identical	yíyàng	一樣	37
ill	bìng	病	32
illness	bìng	病	32

I'm sorry	duìbuqǐ	對不起	41
immediately	lìkè	立刻	46
Imperial Palace	gùgōng	故宮	41
improve	tígāo	提高	36
in a low voice	xiǎoshēng	小聲	46
in loud voice	dàshēng	大聲	34
in the past	yǐqián	以前	32
in whispers	xiǎoshēng	小聲	46
increase	tígāo	提高	36
injection	zhēn	針	46
intelligent	cōngming	聰明	39
intersection	lùkǒu	路口	38
international	guójì	國際	31
it	tā	它	44
it doesn't matter	méiguānxi	沒關系	41
it is said that	tīngshuō	聽説	41
item	jiémù	節目	49

j

jade	yù	玉	36
job	huór	活兒	42
jujube tree	zǎoshù	棗樹	47
jump	tiào	跳	44
just	cái	才	41
just	gāng	剛	38

k

keep	bǎochí	保持	40
kill	shā	殺	49
kilogram	gōngjīn	公斤	42
kind	qīnqiè	親切	43
kind/sort	zhǒng	種	36
knock （at a door）	qiāo	敲	33
knowledge	zhīshi	知識	32
Kunming Lake	Kūnmíng Hú	昆明湖	44

l

labor	láodòng	勞動	49
lake	hú	湖	44

lamp	dēng	燈	48
landscape	fēngjǐng	風景	44
landscape garden	yuánlín	園林	44
lane	hútòng	胡同	38
language	yǔyán	語言	31
lantern	dēng	燈	48
lantern	dēnglóng	燈籠	48
Lantern Festival	dēngjié	燈節	48
Lantern Festival	Yuānxiáo Jié	元宵節	48
last	zuìhòu	最後	50
last （time）	shàng（cì）	上（次）	37
lately	zuìjìn	最近	32
later	hòulái	後來	45
lay （the table）	bǎi	擺	48
leaf	yèzi	葉子	33
lean	shòu	瘦	37
least	zuì	最	33
leave hospital	chūyuàn	出院	47
leave a message	liúyán	留言	47
leave one's comments	liúyán	留言	47
leg	tuǐ	腿	45
lend	jiè	借	49
length	chángduǎn	長短	37
let off （firecrackers）	fàng （bàozhú）	放（爆竹）	48
letter box	xìnxiāng	信箱	34
liberate	jiěfàng	解放	36
lid	gàir	蓋兒	42
lie	tǎng	躺	36
life	shēngmìng	生命	32
life	shēnghuó	生活	47
light	dēng	燈	48
light （bright）	liàng	亮	43
like this	zhèyàng	這樣	32
line of verse	jù	句	39
line up	páidùi	排隊	38
lion	shīzi	獅子	42
list	dān	單	34
live	huó	活	47
live	shēnghuó	生活	47
liver	gān	肝	32
living	huó	活	47

local flavor/style	fēngwèi	風味	43
long	cháng	長	31
Long Corridor	Cháng Láng	長廊	44
Longgevity Hill	Wànshòu Shān	萬壽山	44
look out	dāngxīn	當心	43
looks	yàngzi	樣子	45
loose-fitting	féi	肥	37
lose	diū	丢	41
loudly （read, speak, etc.）	dàshēng	大聲	34
love	ài	愛	45
lovely	kě'ài	可愛	45

m

mail	jì	寄	34
mail box	xìnxiāng	信箱	34
make （dumplings）	bāo	包	48
make it convenient	fāngbiàn	方便	42
make money	zhèng	挣	35
make up one's mind	juédìng	决定	44
make use of	lìyòng	利用	35
man	nánzǐ	男子	40
man of letters	wénxuéjiā	文學家	47
manner	yàngzi	樣子	45
manufacture	shēngchǎn	生產	36
marble pillar（ornamental column in front of palaces）	huábiǎo	華表	42
mass	qúnzhòng	群衆	47
master worker	shīfu	師傅	43
material	liàozi	料子	37
maternal grandmother	lǎolao	姥姥	46
may	kěnéng	可能	46
meaning	yìsi	意思	39
measure	liáng	量	32
medical department	nèikē	内科	32
medicine	yào	藥	46
menu	càidān	菜單	43
meter （a measure word）	mǐ	米	37
middle	zhōngjiān	中間	42
midwinter	lóngdōng	隆冬	33
milk	níunǎi	牛奶	43

mirror	jìngzi	鏡子	44
mist	wù	霧	33
mistake	cuòwù	錯誤	47
model	diǎnxíng	典型	42
modernization	xiàndàihuà	現代化	31
money	qián	錢	35
"Monkey Creates Havoc in Heaven"	Dànàotiāngōng	大鬧天宮	32
Monument to the People	Rénmín Yīngxióng Jìniànbēi	人民英雄紀念碑	42
most	zuì	最	33
motorcycle	mótuōchē	摩托車	41
mother	mǔqin	母親	44
mountain	shān	山	41
mouth	zuǐ	嘴	32
move	bān	搬	42
move	dòng	動	42
move	gǎndòng	感動	49
moving	gǎndòng	感動	49
Museum of Chinese History	Zhōngguó Lìshǐ Bówùguǎn	中國歷史博物館	42

n

National Art Gallery	Zhōngguó Měishù Guǎn	中國美術館	50
native	běn	本	34
near	jìn	近	44
neat	zhěngqí	整齊	48
needle	zhēn	針	46
neighbor	línjū	鄰居	39
new term begins	kāixué	開學	35
New Year	xīnnián	新年	48
New Year (or Spring Festival) picture	niánhuàr	年畫兒	48
New Year's Eve	chúxī	除夕	48
New Year's Eve dinner	niányèfàn	年夜飯	48
New Year scrolls	chūnlián	春聯	39
next (week)	xià (xīngqī)	下（星期）	37
nice & cold	liángkuai	涼快	33
nice & warm	nuǎnhuo	暖和	33
no sooner than	yī...jiù...	一...就...	39

normal	zhèngcháng	正常	32
north	běibiān	北邊	47
northen part	běibiān	北邊	47
nose	bízi	鼻子	32
not only... but also	búdàn...érqiě	不但…而且…	49
not...until	cái	才	41
notebook	běnzi	本子	39
novel	xiǎoshuō	小說	41
nurse	hùshì	護士	46

O

office	bàngōngshì	辦公室	42
old	lǎo	老	31
old steed in the stable still aspires to gallop a thousand li; (fig.) old people may still cherish high aspirations	lǎojìfúlì zhìzàiqiānlǐ	老驥伏櫪志在千里	39
one of...	...zhīyī	…之一	49
one's own	běn	本	34
only	cái	才	41
only	zhǐ	只	36
only	zhǐyǒu	只有	44
only a short while ago	gāng	剛	38
open	dǎkāi	打開	50
opportunity	jīhuì	機會	35
or	yàobù	要不	37
or else	yàobù	要不	37
orchid	lánhuā	蘭花	50
order	dìngzuò	定作	37
ordinary mail	píngxìn	平信	34
other	biéde	別的	43
other people	biérén	別人	36
others	biérén	別人	36
outside	miànr	面兒	37
overcast sky	yītiān	陰天	33
overseas Chinese	huáqiáo	華僑	31
ox	niú	牛	47

P

pacel	bāoguǒ	包裹	39
page	yè	頁	50
pagoda	tǎ	塔	44
pain	téng	疼	46
painting	huàr	畫兒	36
panda	xióngmāo	熊猫	45
panda exhibition hall	xióngmāoguǎn	熊猫館	45
park	gōngyuán	公園	33
parking lot (for bicycles)	cúnchēchù	存車處	43
pass away	shìshì	逝世	50
pass by	guò	過	41
passport	hùzhào	護照	31
paste	tiē	貼	48
patient	bìngrén	病人	46
pavilion	tíngzi	亭子	41
pay (money)	jiāo	交	37
pay a New year call	bàinián	拜年	48
pea gruel	wǎndòuzhōu	豌豆粥	43
people	qúnzhòng	群衆	47
perform	yǎn	演	49
perform	yǎnchū	演出	49
performance	yǎnchū	演出	49
performer	yǎnyuán	演員	49
pharmacist	yàojìshī	藥劑士	46
photograph	túpiàn	圖片	34
physical examination	jiǎnchá	檢查	32
picture	huàr	畫兒	36
picture	túpiàn	圖片	34
place	dìfang	地方	32
place (as verb)	fàng	放	34
place (a measure word)	míng	名	40
plant (as verb)	zhòng	種	46
plate	páizi	牌子	34
platform	zhǔxítái	主席台	40
play (e.g. in movies)	yǎn	演	49
play (string instruments)	lā	拉	31
player (in sports)	yùndòngyuán	運動員	40
pleasantly cool	liángkuai	凉快	33
plum blossom	méihuā	梅花	33
plump	pàng	胖	37
pneumonia	fèiyán	肺炎	32

poem	shī	詩	33
poetry	shī	詩	33
point at/to	zhǐ	指	34
point of time	shíjiān	時間	31
porcelain	cíqì	瓷器	36
possible	kěnéng	可能	46
post	jì	寄	34
post office	yóujú	郵局	34
post-office box	xìnxiāng	信箱	34
postcard	mínxìnpiàn	明信片	34
pot （a measure word）	hú	壺	36
precious	zhēnguì	珍貴	45
premier	zǒnglǐ	總理	50
Premier Zhou	Zhōu Zǒnglǐ	周總理	50
prescription	yàofāng	藥方	46
present	lǐwù	禮物	48
previous （occasion）	shàng（cì）	上（次）	37
price	jiàqián	價錢	36
probable	kěnéng	可能	46
produce	shēngchǎn	生產	36
programme	jiémù	節目	49
public	gōnggòng	公共	38
push	tuī	推	43
put	bǎi	擺	48
put	fàng	放	34
put forward	tí	提	43
put in order	shōushi	收拾	48
put on a show	yǎnchū	演出	49
put somebody to trouble	máfan	麻煩	48
put up	guà	掛	34

q

quality	zhìliàng	質量	36
quite	bǐjiào	比較	43

r

rabbit	tùzi	兔子	48
radio	shōuyīnjī	收音機	48
radio（/wire-broadcasting） announcer	guǎngbōyuán	廣播員	41

rain	yǔ	雨	33
rain (as verb)	xià (yǔ)	下(雨)	33
raincoat	yǔyī	雨衣	37
realize	shíxiàn	實現	31
receipt	shōujù	收據	34
receive	shōu	收	34
recently	zuìjìn	最近	32
record	jìlù	記録	40
record	lùyīn	録音	46
recording	lùyīn	録音	46
recover	huīfù	恢復	47
red autumnal leaves	hóngyè	紅葉	33
red lotus	hónglián	紅蓮	50
rediculous	kěxiào	可笑	45
refreshments	xiǎochī	小吃	43
regard as	zuò	作	47
register (a letter, etc)	guàhào	掛號	34
register card	guàhàozhèng	掛號證	46
regular	zhèngcháng	正常	32
relieve oneself	jiě	解	46
remain	liú	留	39
remember	jì	記	39
repair	xiū	修	38
respectively	gè	各	43
restaurant	fànguǎn	飯館	43
result	chéngjī	成績	35
retain	bǎochí	保持	40
retire	tuìxiū	退休	39
reunite	tuánjù	團聚	48
rich	fēngfù	豐富	47
ride (a bycicle)	qí	騎	37
right	zhèngquè	正確	49
road	lù	路	31
road	mǎlù	馬路	38
rock	shí (tou)	石(頭)	42
rostrum	zhǔxítái	主席台	40
ruin the effect by adding what is superfluous (fig)	huàshétiānzú	畫蛇添足	36
ruler	chǐ	尺	42
run	pǎo	跑	37

S

sack	dài	袋	48
same	yíyàng	一樣	37
scenery	fēngjǐng	風景	44
school	xuéxiào	學校	31
school begins	kāixué	開學	35
sea	hǎi	海	50
seat	zuòwèi	座位	38
second（a measure word）	miǎo	秒	40
see （a doctor）	kàn（bìng）	看（病）	35
sell	mài	賣	49
semester	xuéqī	學期	35
sentence	jù	句	39
serious	lìhài	厲害	46
serve	fúwù	服務	43
set（a meassure word）	tào	套	36
shadowbox	dǎ（quán）	打（拳）	40
Shanghai	Shànghǎi	上海	31
shop	diàn	店	43
shop assistant	shòuhuòyuán	售貨員	36
shop assistant	yíngyèyuán	營業員	34
shopkeeper	zhǎnggui	掌櫃	49
short	duǎn	短	37
short note	tiáozi	條子	39
short story	xiǎoshuō	小説	41
shout	hǎn	喊	44
show	yǎnchū	演出	49
shut	guān	關	46
side	biān	邊	44
sign	jī	迹	33
sign	páizi	牌子	34
silk fabric	chóuzi	綢（子）	37
simple & unadorned	jiǎnpǔ	簡樸	47
situation	qíngkuàng	情況	35
sky	tiān	天	44
slip of paper	tiáozi	條子	39
smile	wēixiào	微笑	50
snack	xiǎochī	小吃	43
snack bar	xiǎochīdiàn	小吃店	43
snow	xuě	雪	33

so	suǒyǐ	所以	44
so	zhème	這麼	42
so	zhèyàng	這樣	32
socialism	shèhuìzhǔyì	社會主義	31
society	shèhuì	社會	49
socks	wàzi	襪子	37
solo	dúchàng	獨唱	43
some	yǒude	有的	34
son	érzi	兒子	48
soprano	nǚgāoyīn	女高音	49
sore	téng	疼	46
south	nānbiān	南邊	38
South Asia	Nān Yà	南亞	45
southern part	nānbiān	南邊	38
spectator	guānzhòng	觀衆	40
speak	jiǎng	講	38
specialized subject	zhuānyè	專業	35
specialty	zhuānyè	專業	35
spend one's holidays	dùjià	度假	44
spoken drama	huàjù	話劇	49
sport	yùndòng	運動	40
sports meet	yùdònghuì	運動會	40
sportsground	cāochǎng	操場	40
sportsman	yùndòngyuán	運動員	40
spring	chūntiān	春天	39
Spring Festival	chūnjié	春節	48
Spring Festival couplets	chūnlián	春聯	39
squad	bān	班	42
square	guǎngchǎng	廣場	41
square meter	pīngfāngmǐ	平方米	42
squeeze	jǐ	擠	41
stamp	yóupiào	郵票	34
stand	lì	立	33
stand erect/upright	tǐnglì	挺立	50
state of affairs	qíngkuàng	情況	35
statue	gèzi	個子	32
stockings	wàzi	襪子	37
stomach	wèi	胃	32
stone	shí（tou）	石（頭）	42
stool	dàbiàn	大便	46
stop（said of bus, etc.）	zhàn	站	38

store	diàn	店	43
story	gùshi	故事	38
stout	pàng	胖	37
street	mǎlù	馬路	38
street	jiē	街	39
strange	qíguài	奇怪	35
subscribe to	dìng	訂	36
subway	dìtiě	地鐵	38
succeed	chénggōng	成功	49
such	zhème	這麼	42
such	zhèyàng	這樣	32
sufficient	gòu	够	43
sugar	táng	糖	43
suggest	tí	提	43
Summer Palace	Yíhéyuán	頤和園	33
summer vocation	shǔjià	暑假	35
sun	tàiyáng	太陽	44
sunglasses	mòjìng	墨鏡	45
surprised	qíguài	奇怪	35
surrender	qūfú	屈服	33
sweep	sǎo	掃	48
sweet dumplings made of glutinous rice flour	yuánxiāo	元宵	43
synopsis	shuōmíngshū	説明書	49

t

tablet (a measure word)	piàn	片	46
tail	wěiba	尾巴	47
take	ná	拿	32
take (along)	dài	帶	38
take away	bān	搬	42
take care	dāngxīn	當心	43
take somebody as	zuò	作	47
take X-ray examination	tòushì	透視	32
talk	huà	話	31
tall	gāo	高	37
Tangshan	Tángshān	唐山	36
tasty	hǎochī	好吃	43
taxi	chūzūqìchē	出租汽車	38
tea service/set	chájù	茶具	36

teacup	cháwǎn	茶碗	36
teahouse	cháguǎn	茶館	49
teapot	cháhú	茶壺	36
telegram	diànbào	電報	34
tell	jiǎng	講	38
ten thousand	wàn	萬	42
term	xuéqī	學期	35
terminal point	zhōngdiǎn	終點	38
terminus	zhōngdiǎn	終點	38
terrible	lìhai	厲害	46
test （as verb）	kǎo	考	35
test	kǎoshì	考試	35
theatre	jùchǎng	劇場	49
there is no need to	búyòng	不用	31
there is something wrong with	huài	壞	49
therefore	suǒyǐ	所以	44
they（for things/animals）	tāmen	它們	44
thick	hòu	厚	36
thin	shòu	瘦	37
thin	báo	薄	34
thing	dōngxi	東西	30
think	juéde	覺得	33
think of	huáiniàn	懷念	47
thirsty	kě	渴	43
this	běn	本	34
though	suīrán	雖然	39
thoughtful	zhōudào	周到	41
thousand	qiān	千	42
Tian'anmen （Gate of Heavenly Peace）	Tiān'ānmén	天安門	34
Tian'anmen Square	Tiān'ānmén Guǎngchǎng	天安門廣場	41
ticket office	shòupiàochù	售票處	41
ticket seller	shòupiàoyuán	售票員	38
tidy	zhěngqí	整齊	48
tidy up	shōushi	收拾	48
tiger	lǎohǔ	老虎	47
tight	shòu	瘦	37
time （a measure word）	cì	次	31
to	duì	對	39

to the highest/lowest degree	zuì	最	33
touch (one's feeling)	gǎndòng	感動	49
toward	wàng	往	33
trace	jī	迹	33
track	jī	迹	33
trade	màoyì	貿易	44
traditional Chinese calendar	xiàlì	夏歷	48
traffic light/signal	hónglǜdēng	紅綠燈	38
travel	lǚxíng	旅行	44
tree	shù	樹	33
troublesome	máfan	麻煩	48
turn a corner	guǎiwān	拐彎	38
turn into	chéng	成	47
type/kind	zhǒng	種	36
typical	diǎnxíng	典型	42

u

uncle	dàye	大爺	38
uncle (father's younger brother)	shūshu	叔叔	39
under	xiàbiān	下邊	34
underground	dìtiě	地鐵	38
underneath	xiàbiān	下邊	34
United States of America	měiguó	美國	31
university	dàxué	大學	31

v

vacation	jiàqī	假期	35
valuable	zhēnguì	珍貴	45
vanish	jué	絶	33
various	gè	各	43
verse	shī	詩	33
violin	xiǎotíqín	小提琴	31
visitor	kèren	客人	39
visitors' book	liúyánbù	留言簿	47

w

wall	qiáng	牆	34
ward (of a hospital)	bìngfáng	病房	46

wardrobe	yīguì	衣櫃	39
warm	nuǎnhuo	暖和	33
warm	rèliè	熱烈	40
wash	xǐ	洗	41
way	lù	路	31
we	zǎnmen	咱們	38
wear (cap/glasses/gloves)	dài	戴	45
weather	tiānqì	天氣	31
welcome	huányíng	歡迎	38
west	xībiān	西邊	41
western part	xībiān	西邊	41
Wester-style suit	xīzhuāng	西裝	37
what	duōme	多麽	44
whole	quán	全	48
why	zěnme	怎麽	38
why	wèishénme	爲什麽	34
wide	kuān	寬	42
wind	fēng	風	33
window	chuānghu	窗户	44
window	chuāngkǒu	窗口	34
winter jasmine	yíngchūnhuā	迎春花	50
winter vocation	hánjià	寒假	35
wish (as noun & verb)	xíwàng	希望	31
wish somebody a happy New Year	bàinián	拜年	48
with much toil	xīnkǔ	辛苦	31
woollen sweater	máoyī	毛衣	37
words	huà	話	31
work	gàn	幹	42
work	láodòng	勞動	49
work	huór	活兒	42
works (of literature/art)	zuòpǐn	作品	49
workshop	chējiān	車間	39
world	shìjiè	世界	50
wrap	bāo	包	48
wrist watch	biǎo	表	35
writer	wénxuéjiā	文學家	47
writings	wénzhāng	文章	47
wrong	chuò	錯	38

y

yield	qūfú	屈服	33
youth	qīngnián	青年	47

z

zero	líng	零	36
Zhou Enlai	Zhōu Ēnlái	周恩來	50
zoo	dòngwùyuán	動物園	45

Appendix III

(Stroke Number)

Character	Pinyin
2	
了	liǎo
3	
之	zhī
下	xià
山	shān
才	cái
千	qiān
4	
天	tiān
片	piàn
分	fēn
牛	niú
尺	chǐ
手	shǒu
比	bǐ
公	gōng
毛	máo
内	nèi
方	fāng
司	sī
已	yǐ
元	yuán
5	
立	lì
市	shì
它	tā
玉	yù
本	běn
古	gǔ
布	bù
只	zhǐ
叫	jiào
出	chū
生	shēng
包	bāo
句	jù
北	běi
片	piàn
石	shí
平	píng
世	shì
打	dǎ
主	zhǔ
永	yǒng
6	
交	jiāo
米	mǐ
次	cì
死	sǐ
百	bǎi
成	chéng
考	kǎo
地	dè
老	lǎo
灰	huī
吊	diào
丢	diū
竹	zhú
年	nián
先	xiān
血	xuè
各	gè

全 quán
收 shōu
耳 ěr
合 hé
决 jué
冰 bīng
存 cún
江 jiāng
自 zì
西 xī
因 yīn

7

彷 páng
完 wán
冷 lěng
初 chū
抓 zhuā
把 bǎ
作 zuò
肝 gān
改 gǎi
但 dàn
豆 dòu
利 lì
李 lǐ
社 shè
汽 qì
希 xī
辛 xīn
杏 xìng
尾 wěi

8

所 suǒ
使 shǐ
放 fàng
雨 yǔ
表 biǎo
青 qīng
長 cháng
枝 zhī
拉 lā
往 wǎng
肥 féi
爬 pá
怕 pà
阿 ā
東 dōng
拐 guǎi
阜 fù
近 jìn
肺 fèi
刮 guā
屈 qū
昆 kūn
周 zhōu
油 yóu
奇 qí
叔 shū

9

洗 xǐ
活 huó
首 shǒu
美 měi
訂 dìng
度 dù
亮 liàng
頁 yè
封 fēng
掙 zhèng
指 zhǐ
厚 hòu
胃 wèi
秒 miǎo
重 zhòng
風 fēng
科 kē
胖 pàng

拜 bài
保 bǎo
便 biàn
查 chá
春 chūn
咳 ké
恢 huī
胡 hú
南 nán
故 gù
皇 huāng
亭 tíng
兔 tù
亞 yà
炸 zhǎ
甚 shén
修 xiū
珍 zhēn
建 jiàn

10

座 zuò
站 zhàn
記 jì
病 bìng
疼 téng
被 bèi
高 gāo
海 hǎi
班 bān
草 cǎo
套 tào
株 zhū
剛 gāng
借 jiè
針 zhēn
拿 ná
迹 jī
退 tuì
航 háng
料 liào
涼 liáng
旅 lǚ
馬 mǎ
唐 táng
除 chú

11

得 dé
寄 jì
帶 dài
雪 xuě
接 jiē
推 tuī
掃 sǎo
掛 guà
累 lèi
船 chuān
貨 huò
袋 dài
第 dì
動 dòng
够 gòu
脚 jiǎo
彩 cǎi
畢 bì
假 jià
連 lián
透 tòu
梅 méi
麻 má
培 péi
設 shè
逝 shì
探 tàn
偉 wěi
野 yě
眼 yǎn
專 zhuān
終 zhōng

陰	yīn
黃	huáng
換	huàn
郵	yóu
瓷	cí
殺	shā

12

衆	zhòng
華	huá
壺	hú
湖	hú
渴	kě
著	zhe
提	tí
晴	qíng
短	duǎn
象	xiàng
最	zuì
量	liáng
跑	pǎo
單	dān
貼	tiē
幅	fú
喊	hǎn
街	jiē
粥	zhōu
菜	cài
絶	jué
景	jǐng
寒	hán
隆	lóng
勞	láo
牌	pái
舒	shū
痛	tòng
陽	yáng
暑	shǔ
掌	zhǎng
愉	yú
棗	zǎo
棉	mián
發	fā

13

詩	shī
話	huà
填	tián
塔	tǎ
萬	wàn
搬	bān
幹	gàn
碗	wǎn
零	líng
路	lù
跳	tiào
節	jié
解	jiě
逼	bī
遍	biàn
過	guò
塊	kuài
當	dāng
暖	nuǎn
聖	shèng
爺	yé
運	yùn
葉	yè
微	wēi
預	yù
群	qún

14

裹	guǒ
演	yǎn
敲	qiāo
種	zhǒng
綢	chóu
鼻	bí
廣	guǎng

蓋 gài
腿 tuǐ
旗 qí
僑 qiáo
熊 xióng
獎 jiǎng
實 shí
慣 guàn
餃 jiǎo

15

瘦 shòu
寬 kuān
養 yǎng
熱 rè
賣 mài
輛 liàng
篇 piān
躺 tǎng
價 jià
餓 è
緞 duàn
鄰 lín
摩 mó
樣 yàng
厲 lì
鞋 xié
摹 mó
墨 mò

16

糖 táng
燈 dēng
頭 tóu
樹 shù
橋 qiáo
嘴 zuǐ
錯 cuò
錢 qián
操 cāo
獨 dú
機 jī
激 jī
歷 lì
辦 bàn
駱 luò
鋼 gāng
遺 yí
頤 yí
選 xuǎn

17

績 jī
講 jiǎng
擠 jǐ
薄 báo
騎 qí
牆 qiáng
聰 cōng
檢 jiǎn
雖 suí

18

戴 dài
禮 lǐ
櫃 guì
醫 yī
霧 wù
藍 lán
擺 bǎi
簡 jiǎn
臨 lín

19

嚮 xiàng
邊 biān
藥 yào
壞 huài
爆 bào

鏡	jìng
懷	huái
關	guān
藝	yì

20

鐘	zhōng
覺	jué

21

顧	gù
蘭	lán
護	hù

23

體	tǐ
臟	zàng

24

讓	ràng

25

觀	guān